W9-BXX-206

AMERICAN POWER

STILL THE BEST HOPE FOR PEACE

CRAIG NELSON CARUANA

Copyright © 2011 by Craig N. Caruana

Published in the United States by Pax Americana Institute.
All rights reserved.
Printed in the United States of America.

No part of this book may be reproduced in any manner
whatsoever without written permission except in the case
of brief quotations or citations embodied in critical articles
and reviews. For information, address The Pax Americana
Institute, 6666 Odana Road, PMB #518, Madison,
Wisconsin 53719. Pax Americana Institute books are
available at special discounts for bulk purchases in the
United States by universities, think-tanks, corporations,
and other organizations. For special information, please
contact the Marketing Division of the Pax Americana
Institute, 6666 Odana Road, PMB #518, Madison, WI
53719, or email info@paxamericanainstitute.org

ISBN #: 978-1-105-67480-8
Content ID: 12799041
Book Title: American Power: Still the Best Hope for Peace
Cover photo: American servicemen and women gather in
front of 'Rainbow Corner' Red Cross club in Paris to
celebrate the unconditional surrender of the Japanese.
By McNulty, August 15, 1945
National Archives and Records Administration, Records of
the Office of the Chief Signal Officer (111-SC-210241)
[VENDOR # 107]

AKNOWLEDGEMENTS

I would like to thank the Pax Americana Institute for publishing *American Power: Still the Best Hope for Peace.* PAI's Executive Director Drew Davis first gave me the opportunity to write as the PAI's National Security Fellow and then graciously accepted my book proposal. Deputy Policy Director Christopher Schaefer thoroughly analyzed my very rough drafts and made recommendations which vastly improved my work. Contributing Fellow Todd Searle provided valuable research as did PAI interns Archana Vuyyuru and Michael Hopfensperger.

I would also like to thank Patrick McGuire, Maureen McGough Wolcott and Daniel Bulger for reading through early drafts and helping to keep the book clear and concise. My thanks also go to Broderick Morgan and Gregory Stevenson for smoothing over the rougher edges of the final drafts.

Many of the thoughts and ideas expressed in this book originated while I earned my master's degree from The George H. W. Bush School of Government and Public Service at Texas A&M University. In place of a traditional thesis, I along with a team of graduate students conducted a study for the National Intelligence Council and the State Department. While preparing for our briefings, I seriously began to think about writing this book. The education I received was an invaluable contribution and this book would not exist had I not spent time at the Bush School.

Finally, I would like to thank my parents Karen and Lawrence Caruana for turning so many of the thoughts in my head into reality.

TABLE OF CONTENTS

MY PURPOSE..1-7

ONE: THE VERSAILLES SYSTEM FAILS......................8-27

TWO: A SECOND CHANCE..28-48

THREE: THE AMERICAN SYSTEM WINS...................49-71

FOUR: THE AMERICAN SYSTEM SPREADS................72-96

FIVE: THE ONCE AND FUTURE GUARDIAN...............97-125

NOTES AND BIBLIOGRAPHY.....................................i-xxx

MY PURPOSE

Security is the most valuable commodity on the international market. As former Assistant Secretary of State Joseph Nye wrote, "Security is like oxygen-you tend not to notice it until you begin to lose it, but once that occurs there is nothing else that you will think about."[1] Around the world American military power allows most nations to breathe easier.

The purpose of this book is to explain to the American people the unique and important role the United States fulfills internationally. The mistakes at Versailles, the triumphs of the Marshall Plan, the Cold War and conflicts in the Persian Gulf are well known to American citizens; however comprehending these events in terms of the systematic success or failure of global order is usually confined to the conversations of academics. This book attempts to shed light on how and why the United States is the guardian of an international system which makes war between great powers less rather than more likely.

Could Europe ever again be at war with itself? The answer amongst my European friends is an emphatic *No!* Indeed, how could such a question even be asked given decades of peace on the continent? At the same time, the younger generation of Europeans cannot understand why American troops remain in Europe. In their opinion the continent would get along just fine without an American military presence.

This conversation took place in Lyon, France, a city close to the Alps and the border with Switzerland. Lyon is a proper setting for such a discussion considering the city was the center of the French resistance during the Second World War. The last time the United States left Europe to manage its own security affairs was in 1919 at the end of what was then known as The Great War (World War I). Within a generation France was conquered and subjugated by German armies. Men motivated to shout *"Heil Hitler!"* conquered whatever force could be marshaled by General Maurice Gamelin fighting for liberté, égalité and fraternité. It has been over sixty-five years since France and most of Europe descended into a barbaric darkness at the hands of Nazi invaders and twenty years since the conclusion of the Cold War when an iron curtain was lifted from a divided continent. For many Europeans these names, terms and events are safely confined to the pages of history never to be experienced again.

The conversation I took part in six months earlier in Doha, Qatar had a different tone. Located in a less than tranquil neighborhood, Qatar's neighbors are Saudi Arabia and Iran. A well connected Qatari citizen in the energy industry told my group of graduate students that after discovering the largest liquefied natural gas (LNG) reserves in the world, Qatar had a choice – make a deal either with the Americans or the Iranians. The Qataris chose the United States. The United States government provides security for Qatari energy while American companies deliver LNG on the world market. In exchange the Qatari government allows the American military to operate from Qatar, which is now home to U.S. Central Command – the American military headquarters for the Middle East. Unlike Europe, the Middle East remains enmeshed in traditional historic struggles and all the barbarism which accompanies war. In this region security is precarious and in constant need of reassurance.

Europe consumes our past, the Middle East our present, but it will be in East Asia where the story of the 21st century is written. In 2006, I had the honor of standing on the White House lawn for China's President Hu Jintao's visit with President George W. Bush. About ninety seconds into

Hu's speech, a member of the Falun Gong began heckling
him. It served as a reminder that although neither side may
want confrontation, there are plenty of issues the United
States and China disagree about. China has steadily
increased its wealth since it opened its economy and joined
the American led international system in the late 1970s.
With money comes power. The two are intertwined, one
used to accumulate more of the other. How China uses its
ever increasing strength will have a significant impact on the
international system of nations.

For over sixty-five years the United States of
America has been the guardian of the international system.
The main virtues of this system—respect for national
sovereignty and economic openness—are not simply the
natural features of international relations; rather, they have
become the norms of behavior in an American designed
global order.[2] The United States is able to sustain this
system because it is capable and willing to fight and win wars
in any region of the world. This fact has deterred would be
aggressors from coercing and attacking nations allied with
the United States. The success of this system is most acute
in Europe, East Asia and the Middle East. The fact that the
leading powers of the world do not engage in war against

each other is a significant achievement. This is not just happenstance, but rather a direct result of American power. Should the United States cease this role or be unable to fulfill its obligations, the world would once again descend into conflict.

Recent books have sought to capture the changing dynamics of global order. Fareed Zakaria's *The Post American World* discusses what the rise of new powers means for the United States and its influence in the world. Parag Khanna's *The Second World: How Emerging Powers Are Redefining Global Competition in the Twenty-first Century*, makes the argument that the world is now interconnected and power will be split relatively among the three empires: the United States, China and Europe. Thomas L. Friedman and Michael Mandelbaum's *That Used To Be Us: How America Fell Behind In The World It Invented and How We Can Come Back*, explains how the United States is slowly declining and offers recommendations for the country to regain its competitive edge in the world. Similar to these books, *American Power* is a discussion about the United States' role in the world. However, different from the aforementioned works, *American Power* does not present an all-encompassing argument to explain *everything* that is happening in the world. Rather, *American Power* focuses on how and why the United States plays an active role in the security of Europe, East Asia and the Middle East. This book makes the argument that the United States' involvement in these regions has prevented a recurrence of great power war.

While it is widely accepted that there are broad economic changes underway, the political implications of this transition are not fully appreciated. War, especially war between great powers, is a horrific endeavor. Through a combination of choice and fate, the United States is responsible for maintaining peace between great powers in the 21st century.

This book should serve as a reminder that peace between leading economic powers is not common and must not be taken for granted. If the United States is going to succeed in this mission the American public must understand and appreciate the impact American power has on the world. All too often, the big picture gets lost in a world of blog posts, news segments and a continual flow of information which often lacks context and substance. Some ideas are worth more than a bullet point's worth of space. That being said, several of the subjects addressed here could be books themselves. Since *American Power* covers a hundred years of history some aspects of arguments must be left out in the name of space. If security is the most valuable commodity, time is certainly a close runner up. In the interest of the reader's time I kept it short. Enjoy.

Craig Nelson Caruana
Queens, New York
9 May 2012

CHAPTER ONE

THE VERSAILLES SYSTEM FAILS

Comprehending the failure to establish a sustainable global order after the First World War is essential to understanding the international system of the 21st century. The foundation of the international system created in 1919 at Versailles, France was rooted in false assumptions about international relations. The Treaty of Versailles abandoned balance of power logic as a cornerstone of continental security in favor of the harmonious ideas of self-determination and collective security through the power of public opinion.[1] From the 17th century until the early 20th century a rough balance of power existed among the nations of Europe. No single nation was allowed to become too powerful and dominate the continent. For example, when Napoleon Bonaparte attempted to conquer Europe, he was countered by a coalition of nations. Even after his defeat, France was allowed to exist so as to maintain equilibrium of power between the nations of Europe.[2] While this system succeeded in its goal of preserving the existence of states, all too often it did not preserve the peace.

When President Woodrow Wilson headed to Versailles, France to negotiate the end of the Great War, he intended not just to find a settlement to the current conflict; he intended to end the balance of power system which he believed caused war. Wilson led the United States into the Great War for reasons beyond European politics. He asked Congress for a declaration of war against Germany, describing the cause in near apocalyptic terms, "It is a fearful thing to lead this great peaceful people into war, into the most terrible and disastrous of all wars, *civilization itself* seeming to be in the balance."[3] In January 1918, Wilson described his vision for a new world order based, "not a balance of power, but a community of power; not organized rivalries, but an organized common peace."[4] Managing this new global order would be a League of Nations capable of managing the disputes of mankind in a civilized fashion. Wilson believed that international public opinion had the *power* to influence nations.[5] As President, Wilson himself described, "the league of nations is just this, that it shall operate as the organized moral force of men throughout the world, and that whenever or wherever wrong and aggression are planned or contemplated, this searching light of conscience will be turned upon them and men everywhere

will ask, 'What are the purposes that you hold in your heart
against the fortunes of the world?' Just a little exposure will
settle most questions."[6] At Versailles the President achieved
his goal of eliminating the balance of power in Europe, but
unfortunately the absence of balancing left German
revisionist desires unchecked.

German passions stirred with anger at the Treaty of
Versailles' provisions. The Treaty confiscated German
territory, resources and worst of all forced Germany to
accept responsibility for the war – an insult to their honor.[7]
Having just fought a war which saw the use of mustard gas
and other diabolical inventions, it is easy to believe all sides
shared a universal interest in peace. However, Germany
would eventually choose war in place of what it saw as an
unjust peace. The success of the international system created
at Versailles rested on the efficacy of collective security
which held as its sword the virtue of public opinion. While
debating the Versailles Treaty in the House of Commons,
Lord Robert Cecil unintentionally made the ominous
prediction that, "For the most part there is no attempt to rely
on anything like a superstate; no attempt to rely upon force
to carry out a decision of the Council or the Assembly of the
League. That is almost impracticable as things stand now.

What we rely upon is public opinion…and if we are wrong about it, then the whole thing is wrong."[8] It was just a matter of time before Europe would face another crisis.

THE FOUNDATIONS FOR PEACE

Having to live next door to mortal danger, France under the leadership of Prime Minister George Clemenceau argued for a Treaty which would limit German power as much as possible. While all sides suffered from 1914 to 1918, the French had to endure the horrors of battle on their own territory. Out of a country of close to forty million people nearly two million lost their lives defending French soil.[9] Those who were particularly disfigured due to injuries actually had vacation spots set aside for them in rural areas.[10] The 1914 invasion of France was just the latest in a one hundred year struggle with their aggressive neighbor. As Winston Churchill described in his memoirs, "Five times in a hundred years , in 1814, 1815, 1870, 1914, and 1918, had the towers of Notre Dame seen the flash of Prussian guns and heard the thunder of their cannonade."[11] Many of the leaders of France had now survived war twice with the Germans.[12] They were around for the 1870 Franco-Prussian war and had lived with the fear of another invasion for fifty years.[13] André

Tardieu, who was an aide to Clemenceau at Versailles, passionately recalled his country's determination to avoid another German invasion. France "owes it to her people, to the dead who must not have died in vain, to the living who wish to rebuild their country in peace."[14] Finally, in the twilight of their lives, Clemenceau and his countrymen had a chance to put down the German menace for good. Through the Treaty of Versailles, the French sought to establish a balance of power which would dissuade Germany from another war. As insurance, the French wanted a permanent military alliance, including a combined General Staff, with both Great Britain and the United States.[15] Such an alliance would ensure France's survival over the long-term. After barely surviving the last war, the French leadership knew the very existence of their country was at stake. Unfortunately for France, President Wilson did not share his ally's harsh critique of the German problem.

President Wilson believed it was the idea that nations felt the need to balance against each other which had caused so much bloodshed throughout the centuries.[16] The President, who led his country into its first European war, ever, did so to "make the world safe for democracy."[17] He was not about to enter into the centuries old balance of power system of Europe, which was loathsome to American public opinion and contrary to his own views on how nations should conduct international affairs. Underlying this outlook was President Wilson's faulty belief that democracy was going to spread throughout Europe.[18] Therefore, the League of Nations would be perfectly capable of arbitrating international disputes between liberal, civilized countries.

Maintaining peace in the world envisioned by President Wilson and his supporters was just a matter of marshaling the persuasive powers of public opinion.[19] When Lord Cecil addressed the League's first Assembly he again shared his conviction in public opinion, "It is quite true that by far the most powerful weapon at command of the League of Nations is not the economic or the military weapon or any other weapon of material force. By far the strongest weapon we have is the weapon of public opinion."[20] The underlying belief in the power of public opinion rested on the notion that all sides shared the same universal values. This argument was based on President Wilson's view of the benign nature of mankind and the belief that democratic nations will ultimately agree on the fundamentals of right and wrong, even in the complicated realm of international politics.

President Wilson's soaring rhetoric on peace was heard not just in allied nations but in Germany as well. When news of a ceasefire was received, Germans believed President Wilson had made an honest offer for peace and German soldiers were returning home successful in their mission.[21] German civilians on the home front could not conceive of the fact that they had lost the war while their troops still held foreign territory.[22] The revelation of what was about to be imposed upon them inspired revisionist desires in the hearts and minds of every German.

The eventual Treaty forced upon the Germans was reflective not just of Wilsonian principals, but also contained measures favored by France to reduce German power. Germany was required to virtually disarm, pay $5 billion up front to the Allies, provide coal to France, surrender much of its merchant Fleet to Great Britain and even transfer German patents, such as Bayer Aspirin, to the United States.[23] In addition, Germany lost twenty-five thousand square miles of territory which included six million people.[24] Germany also forfeited an extensive amount of its raw materials and its overseas colonies.[25] To add insult to injury, Article 231, which became known as the "War Guilt Clause", forced Germany to accept responsibility for the war.[26] The

Germans viewed this treaty as intolerable. To make matters worse, the new international boundaries of Central Europe were unsustainable.

Without concern for balance of power logic, new states were created out of a hodgepodge of nationalities in Central and Eastern Europe. The Austro-Hungarian Empire had completely disintegrated. Various nationalities suddenly found themselves in newly created countries. Enclaves of ethnic Germans in Czechoslovakia and Poland later became justification by Adolph Hitler to invade these countries. The absence of Russia as a major player in European politics further complicated the balance of power system in Europe.[27] Traditionally, Russia had been a natural ally for France. Any Central European aggressor would face the possibility of a two front war in the event Russia or France was attacked while the two were allied with each other. Unfortunately, the Bolsheivik revolution in Russia produced a government which no longer participated in the great power politics of Europe.[28] British Prime Minister Lloyd George wrote to President Wilson pointing out the problem Versailles had created: "I can not conceive any greater cause of future war than that the German people, who have certainly proved themselves one of the most vigorous and powerful races in the world should be surrounded by a number of small states, many of them consisting of people who have never previously set up a stable government for themselves, but each of them containing large masses of Germans clamouring for reunion with their native land." [29] Thus stood the balance of power on the continent after the Treaty of Versailles - in the center stood sixty-five million Germans knocked down, but not out; to the west only thirty-nine million Frenchmen, exhausted; and to the east countries which were literally born yesterday. The United States avoided security entanglements with yesterday's allies and retreated back across the oceans leaving Europe and the League of Nations to stand on their own. There was no balance - only concentrated power, temporarily but not indefinitely constrained.

ECONOMICS AND WAR

The devastation in manpower, land and materials brought on by the war combined with a failure by the leading powers to work collectively to solve their economic problems added to the political instability of post-war Europe. Prior to the war nations' currencies were on the gold standard -

meaning currencies were fixed to the price of gold. One benefit of the gold standard was minimal transaction costs when money travelled from one country to another. This made it easy for nations to make overseas investments. During the late 19th century, international finance helped facilitate what we now call globalization. The rigidness of the gold standard guaranteed a certain amount of stability in international markets; however it limited the control governments had over their monetary policy. This system existed in a time prior to the ideas of John Maynard Keynes and the need for governments to limit the negative impacts economic recessions can have on individual people. Maintaining this system was the priority for governments. Even if there were negative consequences such high unemployment or reduced economic growth, governments would not abandon the gold standard.[30] However, the First World War shattered the rules concerning this monetary system as it did to so many other international norms. The inability of governments to produce a robust global economy in the post-war world added to the political turmoil engulfing both the vanquished and the victorious alike.

Confronting the need to do everything possible for victory in the war, nations went off the gold standard in order to borrow and print massive sums of money for war needs. It was not easy to go back to the old system once the war concluded. Reparations demanded by the Treaty and repayment of loans muddled an already complicated international finance system.[31] By 1920 world manufacturing production was 7 percent less than a year prior to the war.[32] Agriculture was one-third less than normal.[33] Great Britain, traditionally the manager of international finance proved unable to continue its pre-war role. Although the United States was now the world's leading economy, it failed to take responsibility for the power it had acquired. Given the socio-economic calamity brought on by the war, leadership was lacking at the time it was needed most.[34] As international economic cooperation proved too difficult, governments tried to solve their problems unilaterally, regardless of the overseas effects. During the 1920's tariffs increased around the world.[35] Measures, such as the infamous Smoot-Hawley Act in the United States, helped devolve the world into competing currency blocks.[36] From 1929 when the stock market crashed to 1937 world trade was reduced in half.[37] Each nation tried to gain a competitive advantage at the expense of others.

Under a system where nations try to limit the effects of economic decisions made in foreign capitals, policies which increase a country's autonomy become more attractive. Nations were trying to develop domestic economies which were protected against the actions of foreign governments. Which nations will succeed in such a world? The most successful countries will have access to numerous natural resources and be large in both land and population. The population need not be ethnically homogenous. The only requirement of the population is that it takes orders from a single capital. Countries with these characteristics will be powerful and not need other countries for support. This naturally begs the question, what will nations do if they are not blessed which such fortunate attributes?

Applying the theory expressed above helps shed light on how the nature of the international system during the 1920s and 1930s made another conflict more likely. The United States was already large, populous and filled with natural resources. Therefore, to succeed it did not need more territory. The United States was naturally content with the international status quo. Great Britain, although a small island, had built a vast Empire throughout the centuries. It gave special economic preferences to certain countries, ensuring economic growth and a high living standard for the people of Great Britain. Germany and Japan on the other hand were not satisfied with the status quo. Under this international system Japan needed resources from the East Indies to be a great power. Its small size and reliance on overseas markets was a source of weakness. Only through conquest could Japan be secure.[38] Germany sought to become the dominant land power on the European continent.[39] Only through expanding German territory could Germans be sure they had access to the resources needed for economic growth. In an age of economic turmoil and protectionism, small countries could not rely upon the good will and smart policies of their neighbors. Only brute force could guarantee security.

THE RESULTS OF THE VERSAILLES SYSTEM

If the Versailles Treaty was going to succeed, the victorious powers had to convince the Germans that as bad as the provisions within the Treaty were, the consequences of not abiding by them would be far worse. In this endeavor Great Britain and France completely failed, if it can be said they tried at all. The British and French allowed the Treaty

to be systematically broken and the principals of
international order to be violated. Public opinion revealed
itself an impotent force in international politics.

Italy's invasion of Abyssinia in October 1935 marked
the beginning of the end of the League of Nations as an
actual force in world affairs. In response to this naked
aggression, the League voted for economic sanctions,
however, oil was not included.[40] Great Britain and France
were operating under the notion that by seeking some type of
middle ground Italy would remain an ally against
Germany.[41] In addition, military experts in Great Britain
mistakenly believed that in the time it would take Italy to
conquer Abyssinia the sanctions would dissuade Italy from
continuing the war.[42] This course was a complete failure.
Italy conquered Abyssinia by May of 1936, despite initial
battlefield setbacks. Benito Mussolini, dictator of Italy,
recognized weakness when he saw it.[43] The whole Abyssinia
affair moved Italy closer to Germany.[44] After Abyssinia, it
was clear that the League of Nations did not work. Fifty-two
nations stood in opposition to Italy and used the mechanisms
of the League to stop Italian aggression.[45] The result was
the conquest of Abyssinia and the message to aspiring
powers that history is still moved forward by blood and iron.

British and French feckless responses would continue
as Adolf Hitler reacquired lost territory and invaded his
neighbors. In March 1936, with a force of only 20,000,
Germany occupied the demilitarized Rhineland. Even
without mobilizing, the French army was 500,000 strong. [46]
Had France shown a willingness to confront Hitler the
Germans would have retreated and it is even possible that
Hitler would have been thrown out of power.[47] With
Germany's western flank reoccupied, it was free to improve
its defenses along the border with France. Germany annexed
Austria in 1938 without consequence. Despite these follies,
there was still a chance to confront Germany at a time when
an Allied victory would not have required a long, brutal
struggle.

Hitler's last conquest before the invasion of Poland
was Czechoslovakia. The newly created republic was
formally allied with France. If ever there was a time to show
a willingness to fight it was then. Hitler argued that the
Sudetenland, which was predominately ethnic German,
belonged to Germany. Not only did the Sudetenland border
Germany, but it was well-defended, mountainous territory.
It would have been difficult for the German army to force
itself into Czech territory. This fact was not lost on the

Fuhrer's generals. When Hitler was considering invading Czechoslovakia, Germany's Chiefs of Staff pointed out that Germany's western defenses, the Siegfried Line, was not ready to withstand a French attack. Germany only had thirteen divisions counting reserves to defend its entire western border.[48] France could mobilize a hundred divisions.[49] In addition, it was possible Russia could enter the war due to its cultural ties with the Slavs.[50] Internally, German generals were already laying the foundation for a coup against Hitler should war occur.[51] However, Hitler correctly calculated that Great Britain and France did not have the will to fight. On September 15th 1938, Prime Minister Neville Chamberlain landed in Munich to negotiate a settlement with the Germans. While reviewing the SS troopers, Chamberlain apparently did not see any deeper meaning in the skulls and cross bones which decorated the SS troopers' caps.[52] At the negotiations in Munich, Chamberlain abandoned Czechoslovakia and gave in to Hitler's demands. The Czechoslovak government was forced to surrender its well-defended Sudetenland and soon thereafter their country without firing a shot.

Even once the League of Nations proved ineffective, the British and French had an opportunity to reverse course and use their military might to defeat Hitler with far more ease than they did after war began in 1939. Great Britain and France could have attacked Germany, possibly toppling Hitler from power. During any one of these crises a stronger response in defense of the international system Great Britain and France were trying to establish would have improved the chances of avoiding a long, drawn out European war. However, the system crafted at Versailles was not enforced by the powers which had a stake in its success.

CONCLUSION

The premise of international peace was based on faulty ideas which provided neither political nor economic security. President Wilson's goals were understandable even if his methods were not practical. Great power competition on the European continent had led to numerous wars throughout history. Recognizing the need to change the international system in order to foster a more peaceful coexistence between nations was not naive. However, in crafting a new international system, the statesmen at Versailles, especially President Wilson, would have been wise to realize the virtues of nations balancing against one another. For all its defects, the balance of power system kept one nation from conquering Europe. Just twenty years after this system was abandoned, virtually all of Europe fell under the control of Hitler's Germany. The world was forced to engage in another global war, this one far more disastrous than the first.

The overriding problem for Europe after the First World War was how to handle Germany. The international system created by the Treaty of Versailles required Germany to accept terms and then take action based on those terms, such as reparations and disarmament. If Germany failed to abide by the Treaty, Germany had to be forced to do so by Great Britain, France and the League of Nations. However, as the years went by this became impossible. Great Britain and France did not have the will power to invade Germany and the League of Nations lacked any real efficacy. The Treaty of Versailles created a nation unsatisfied by the status quo with the potential to become the most powerful country on the European continent. The breakup of the Austro-Hungarian empire and the absence of Russia from the political scene created a weak flank to Germany's east. The nature of the balance of power system on the European continent incentivized Germany to seek aggrandizement at the expense of the newly created countries of Slavs, Poles, Czechs and ethnic Germans caught behind arbitrary lines.

The economic order of the world made the political situation even worse. While the horrors of Nazi Germany and Imperial Japan should never be ignored, it is beneficial to understand how the economic aspects of the international system made war more likely. As protectionist measures increased around the world, nations found it difficult to increase their wealth. For powerful nations such as the United States and Great Britain this was unfortunate but tolerable. Indeed, foreign countries were not in a position to push these two behemoths around. However, Germany and Japan were acutely aware of their weaknesses. Under such a system there is a natural incentive for nations to have large swaths of territory and direct control over natural resources. Unfortunately, often the only way to gain such land and material is to seize them through force. Enabling nations to have access to natural resources not under their direct control and the ability to acquire wealth without resorting to force is an essential attribute of a peaceful international system.

The idea that Europe could be brought under the control of a single master was not lost on Allied leaders after the Second World War in 1945. American and British policymakers had learned their lessons well and intended never to repeat the mistakes of the 1919 generation. International systems, however well-constructed, require powerful nations which have a stake in the system to enforce the norms of behavior they wish other nations to abide by. At the end of the Second World War, allied leaders had the opportunity to make the world anew.

CHAPTER TWO

A SECOND CHANCE

The Grand Alliance between Great Britain, the Soviet Union and the United States vanquished the most beastly conquerors the world had ever known. With the demise of Nazism, Fascism and Japanese militarism, the world had a second chance to construct a new international system in the hope that mankind could avoid a third global war. American and British policymakers understood the importance of crafting an international system which eliminated the need for spheres of influence and economic trading blocs.[1] As the British government described before the Potsdam conference, "Our primary objective should be to remove the *causes* which make nations feel that such spheres are necessary to build their security, rather than to assist one country to build up strength against another."[2] The Wilsonian idea of pushing history beyond balance of power concepts endured. Actually constructing a world based on liberal, democratic principles proved just as difficult as during the inter-war years. The Soviet Union had no interest in entering into a new world order based on the values of its ideological opponents.[3]

For the first time after a great power war no single peace settlement was reached.[4] The Allies could not agree on a permanent settlement of how Germany should be treated after the war. Having suffered twenty-seven million casualties, the Soviet Union's strategy to achieve security was to increase their territory into Central Europe, thus creating a buffer between the Russian heartland and the European powers.[5] As the Soviet Foreign Minister Vyacheslav Molotov recalled, "My task as minister of foreign affairs was to expand the borders of our Fatherland...And it seems that Stalin and I coped with this task quite well."[6] Soviet aggrandizement in Eastern Europe, combined with threats to Turkey, Iran and the ongoing civil war in Greece sparked a crisis in Europe. In February 1947, Great Britain announced it could no longer financially afford to support the Greek government in its civil war against communist forces. For centuries a central tenement of British foreign policy was to maintain the balance of power in Europe by allying against whichever nation was seeking to dominate the continent. By ending aid to Greece, Great Britain was announcing it could no longer fulfill its historic role. The third highest ranking official in the State Department, William Clayton recognized that "the reins of world leadership, are fast slipping from Britain's competent but now very weak hands. These reins will be picked up either by the United States or by Russia. If by Russia, there will almost certainly be war in the next decade or so, with the odds against us. If by the United States, war can almost certainly be prevented."[7] The dead were not yet cold and already a third world war was conceivable.

The United States picked up those reins and through its economic, political and military might prevented Western Europe from falling under the totalitarian rule of Joseph Stalin. Only the United States possessed the capacity to stare down the Red Army.[8] Only the United States, not suffering from the destructiveness of battle on its own territory had the economic power to revitalize Western Europe. The decision to use this power did not stem from virtuous values alone, but rather the recognition that if action was not taken, all of Europe would fall under communist and eventually Soviet domination.

ECONOMICS OF PEACE

Through the pain of experience countries knew what type of world they did *not* want to live in. Currency blocs, high tariffs and limited access to resources were the characteristics of a failed international system which helped plunge the world into war. Unfortunately, there was no blueprint on how to create a successful international order. How should the West create a peaceful world after twenty years of war and financial hardship? If the world was to avoid another war, this question had to be answered. Solving the complex financial and economic issues which plagued nations during the inter-war years was not an easy task. The British and Americans had to develop a global economic order which fostered global trade and stabilized currency markets while simultaneously offering protection to domestic industries.[9] Such an arrangement was achieved at the United Nations Monetary and Financial Conference in Bretton Woods, New Hampshire in July 1944. Under the Bretton Woods system, nations pegged their currency to the dollar and the dollar was pegged to gold, thus eliminating the currency fluctuations of the interwar years. At the same time, international institutions were established to offer assistance to countries when economic conditions were poor.

The mechanics of this system lasted until the early 1970s.[10] However, the spirit of nations working together, often through international institutions to solve their economic problems, continues to the present day.

The United States and Great Britain understood that they needed to construct a world order that would foster stability so that nations would not have to live in perpetual fear of conflict. Concern over post-war Europe began even before the United States entered the war. In August 1941, Prime Minister Churchill met President Franklin Delano Roosevelt at sea off the coast of Newfoundland. The two leaders discussed the philosophical foundation upon which the post-war world would be based. The end product produced on August 14th, 1941 was a joint declaration of principles called The Atlantic Charter, which laid out a general foundation for a new international system. Among the Charter's eight points were the following: No nation will seek "aggrandizement"; the right for people to choose their own form of government; cooperation between nations in economics; "access, on equal terms, to the trade and to the raw materials of the world"; freedom of the seas; and finally an idealistic attitude that force as a tool of statecraft should be abandoned and nations must co-exist peacefully.[11] Since the United States was not a belligerent in the war at the time of its creation, the Atlantic Charter was technically just a statement. However, it did provide principals for what the world would look like "after the final destruction of the Nazi tyranny."[12] The new world order would include respect for national sovereignty, open access to natural resources and an open economic system. While these ideas were rooted in Wilsonian philosophy, the United States and Great Britain had the hard lessons of the interwar years teach them the difficulty of implementing such measures. If their vision for the world was going to succeed, Churchill and Roosevelt were going to need the rest of the world, especially the leading economic powers, to be supportive of their ideas and values.

In 1944 representatives from forty-four nations met to develop a framework for managing the international economy once the war concluded. The American sentiment at Bretton Woods can be expressed as, "If goods can't cross borders, soldiers will."[13] Acting on this theory, nations signed the General Agreement on Tariffs and Trade (GATT). This agreement established a mechanism for negotiations to lower trade barriers between nations. GATT culminated with the creation of the World Trade

Organization (WTO) in 1995, which arbitrates and rules on how trade is conducted between nations. It would be decades before nations' economies actually became interdependent upon one another, but the GATT "created a framework for globalization."[14] By allowing countries access to resources needed for economic growth tensions between nations are reduced.

The Bretton Woods Conference also sought to remedy the social upheavals caused by the continuous movement of capital in and out of countries, especially countries with weak domestic institutions.[15] A pillar of international economics and American power in the post-war years was the decision to peg foreign currencies to the U.S. dollar. This eliminated the currency fluctuations of the interwar years allowing for financial stability. The International Monetary Fund (IMF) was established to assist countries that had balance of payment problems and manage exchange rate changes. In addition, individual nations were allowed to restrict the amount of capital flow into and out of their country. If too many imports were wrecking the domestic industries of a nation, the IMF would help finance deficit spending to alleviate domestic social problems. The IMF helped bring stability to international trade and fostered the idea of nations working collectively to solve their economic problems in stark contrast to the "beggar thy neighbor" policies of the interwar years.

Sincere efforts were made by Roosevelt to bring the Soviet Union into the post-war international system envisioned by the United States and Great Britain.[16] During the Bretton Woods conference, the participants decided that the Soviets would be the third most influential nation in the IMF and the World Bank.[17] The Soviet Union was given such a position in spite of the fact that its economy was not a leading driver of international trade. As one participant said, "The quota for the U.S.S.R which was finally agreed upon bore little or no recognition of its importance in world trade and was set almost entirely in recognition of its political and potential economic importance."[18] In this effort not only did the President try to bring the Soviet Union into multilateral institutions, but he also acquiesced to Stalin's demands regarding Poland and the Baltic states. Although Stalin had promised to eventually hold free elections in these countries, he was allowed to install temporary governments which were in line with Moscow's interests. Stalin would eventually break the promises he made at Yalta concerning free elections and the fate of people living in Eastern European countries occupied by the Red Army.[19] Stalin had his own ideas on what was needed for the security of the Soviet Union.

END OF WAR BRINGS NO PEACE

The Soviet Union under the iron fist of Stalin sought to expand Soviet influence as far as the United States and Great Britain would allow.[20] As the preeminent Cold War historian John Lewis Gaddis explains, Stalin saw security only in unilateral terms.[21] It was inconceivable that someone such as Stalin, who survived by massacring his own people, could ever accept a multilateral framework for international security. Stalin viewed international politics the same way he viewed domestic politics – a fight to the death. As Gaddis describes, "World politics was an extension of Soviet politics, which was in turn an extension of Stalin's preferred personal environment: a zero sum game, in which achieving security for one meant depriving everyone else of it."[22] The Soviet Union acquired the Baltic countries and set up communist governments throughout Eastern Europe. The United States policy after the war was not as clear and organized as the totalitarian Soviet Union. Although Great Britain and

the United States knew the type of world order they wanted
to exist, making it happen proved challenging.

If the democracies were going to achieve success,
they needed to create a system that allowed Germany and
Japan to regain economic power while simultaneously avoid a
resumption of security competition in their respective
regions. In the immediate aftermath of the war, the Allies
enacted misguided policies designed to weaken the Axis
powers out of fear that a revived Germany and Japan would
again make war on their neighbors.[23] Germany was broken
apart into different occupation zones amongst the Allies.
The Joint Chiefs of Staff directive 1067 instructed General
Lucius D. Clay, the head of the U.S. military government in
Germany, to "take no steps (a) looking toward the economic
rehabilitation of Germany, or (b) designed to maintain or
strengthen the German economy."[24] The Secretary of the
Treasury, Henry Morgenthau, wanted to go even further
than JCS 1067. Although his ideas were not adopted,
Morgenthau envisioned the complete deindustrialization of
Germany, thus turning the entire country into a society of
farmers.[25] In Japan, General Douglas MacArthur assumed
complete command of the country. Under the U.S. Initial
Post-Surrender Policy (SWNCC 150), General McArthur

was supposed to focus his governance of Japan on de-militarization, punishing war criminals and breaking up Japanese industry associations, known as zaibatsus.[26] Eventually these policies were reversed. Worsening economic and political conditions made it clear to the occupying powers that Germany and Japan had to be rehabilitated if the world was going to be at peace.

The German and Japanese populations suffered heavily from the effects of the war. Over ten million homes were destroyed or severely damaged in Germany.[27] In the Ruher, the industrial heartland of Germany, coal production fell from a pre-war level of 400,000 tons a day to 25,000.[28] During the harsh 1946-47 winter, people living in Germany and the rest of Europe faced the real possibility of starvation.[29] Germans living in the British occupied zone had their rations cut to 1,000 calories a day. In the American zone Germans fared only a little better with 1,160 calories a day.[30] Japan was undergoing a similar situation. Two atomic weapons had been used against civilian populations in addition to the cities destroyed by conventional bombing. In 1946 unemployment stood at 13 million people; industrial production was just a third of the 1934–1936 average; and the media was reporting that people were starving to death.[31]

The fear of a resurgent Germany and Japan was giving way to a fear that these countries would not recover at all. The victorious democracies were losing the peace.

The appeal of communism grew in tandem with the worsening economic conditions in Europe. It is understandable why communism was popular during the post-war era. During the war it was often communists who lead an organized resistance against Nazi occupiers. Now that the war had ended, socio-economic strife plagued war torn nations. Looking back at the inter-war years, capitalism appeared to bring only economic depression and global war. Communism seemingly had the answers to everyone's problems. As historian Melvyn P. Leffler noted communist membership expanded throughout Europe, "The Belgian party grew from 9,000 in 1939 to 100,000 in November 1945; in Holland from 10,000 in 1938 to 53,000 in 1946; in Greece from 17,000 in 1935 to 70,000 in 1945; in Italy from 5,000 in 1943 to 1,700,000 at the end of 1945; in Czechoslovakia from 28,000 in May 1945 to 750,000 in September 1945; in Hungary from a few hundred in 1943 to 100,000 in December 1945. In France, Italy and Finland the Communist vote was already 20 percent of the electorate in 1945."[32] At the same time Soviet foreign policy grew more

menacing to the values expressed in the Atlantic Charter.
The Soviet Union signed bilateral trade agreements with
Poland, Romania, Hungary and Bulgaria.[33] These trade
agreements made it easier for Eastern European countries to
trade with the Soviet Union as opposed to Western Europe.
The materials needed most by Western Europe, such as
grain, meat, coal and oil were even harder to obtain because
of these bilateral treaties. The world was slipping into the
type of trading blocs which helped plunge the world into
war.

The threat and danger of Western Europe falling
under Soviet control cannot be overstated. Just as Eastern
Europe now took orders from Moscow, it was conceivable
that Western Europe would suffer the same fate under
communist governments. Although the Soviet Union was
currently weak, its military potential was enormous. The
United States would not be able to compete with an
economic and military power which controlled all of Eurasia.
As William J. Donovan, the head of the Office of Strategic
Services (which would eventually become the Central
Intelligence Agency) wrote in a memorandum to President
Truman in 1945, if Russia should "succeed in uniting the
resources of Europe and Asia under her sway. Within a

generation Russia could probably then out build us in every phase of military production."[34] There was a real danger that the industrial might of the United States would be surpassed by a Soviet Empire in control of arguably the most important region of the Earth. In such a scenario, the United States would be cut off from the vital resources and markets of Europe. The constant threat of war from a strategically weak position would affect the lives of every citizen. American life would drastically change for the worse.

The Soviet Union's foreign policy only reinforced the Western Allies' fear of Stalin's intentions.[35] Soviet armies continued to occupy northern Iran while at the same time Stalin was demanding new territory from Turkey. Specifically he wanted control over the vital Bosporus and Dardanelles straits. The Soviet Union would then be in a position to threaten the Middle East. The United States responded to Soviet actions by taking the matter to the U.N. Security Council and permanently deploying the U.S. 6th Fleet to the Eastern Mediterranean. However, these were just temporary remedies to a much larger problem. The United States was still not firmly committed to the defense of Western Europe nor did it have a solution for the dire food and housing shortages. Just a few years after the war, the world was reaching another crisis point.

THE BIRTH OF A NEW INTERNATIONAL SYSTEM

President Harry Truman embarked on an ambitious policy of rehabilitating war torn nations while pledging to defend any country against communism. The world reached a crisis point with Great Britain's decision to end aid to Greece in February 1947. This was a pivotal moment for American leadership. Greece is located at the intersection of the Mediterranean Sea and the Middle East – a vital transit area for oil shipments into Europe. The decision was made not only to aid Greece, but to assist any nation facing a security threat from communist forces. Truman went before Congress and proclaimed that it will be "the policy of the United States to support free people who are resisting attempted subjugation by armed minorities or by outside pressures."[36] This pledge of support became known as the Truman Doctrine. However, political and military assistance alone would not solve the socio-economic crisis facing nations devastated by war. Speaking at Baylor University President Truman made the case for a resumption of world trade. "At this particular time, the whole world is concentrating much of its thought and energy on attaining the objectives of peace and freedom. These objectives are bound up completely with a third objective--reestablishment of world trade. In fact the three-peace, freedom, and world trade--are inseparable. The grave lessons of the past have proved it."[37] The only way world trade could begin again was with massive American assistance to Europe.

Poor economic conditions in Europe prevented these nations from having the money to import the equipment necessary to create and maintain a modern economy. Europe was currently undergoing what became known as the "dollar shortage." The only way European countries could grow their economies was with American imports. However, Western European countries were poor. They desperately needed dollars to buy machine tools needed for industry. Speaking at Harvard University, Secretary of State George Marshall described the problem and the need for American aid, "The truth of the matter is that Europe's requirements for the next three or four years of foreign food and other essential products - principally from America - are so much greater than her present ability to pay that she must have substantial additional help or face economic, social, and

political deterioration of a very grave character."[38] To solve
this problem and avoid the "economic, social and political
deterioration" of nations the Marshall Plan provided
approximately $14 billion to Europe.[39] Aid also increased to
Japan doubling to over $404 million in 1947 and totaling
over $1.5 billion.[40] In 1948, total aid to Europe and Japan
was approximately five percent of the United States' GNP.[41]
The economics of Europe were tied to the political question
of what role Germany should play in a post-war Europe.

　　To make the revival of German economic power
more palatable to Great Britain and France, the United
States committed itself to defending Western Europe by
forming the North Atlantic Treaty Organization (NATO).[42]
A similar policy was pursued in Japan. General McArthur
stopped the purging of the zaibatsu. Those that were already
broken up were allowed to reunite.[43] The United States
established military bases throughout Japan and encouraged
foreign trade. In addition, bi-lateral security treaties were
signed with the Philippines, Taiwan, Australia and New
Zeeland. In retrospect these efforts were an enormous
success. Economic growth returned to Western Europe and
communist forces did not seize power. From the beginning
of the Marshall Plan to its conclusion in December 1951, the

GNP of countries receiving assistance grew from $120 billion to $159 billion.[44] Industrial production was 35% higher than in 1938.[45] Food, the basic necessity which was lacking, was up 24% in production compared to 1947 and up 9% compared to prewar levels. [46] Without this assistance Europe would have continued down a path of socio-economic ruin. Instead, Europe turned a page in its history. Multilateral European institutions, such as the Organization for European Economic Cooperation which helped coordinate aid from the Marshall Plan, formed the foundation for what eventually became the European Union.[47] Out of the ashes of war a new system was being created to keep the peace.

The United States did not repeat the mistake of believing defeated countries would accept their status as vanquished belligerents indefinitely. The humanitarian crisis coupled with the threat of international communism motivated the United States to rebuild Germany and Japan. In so doing, the United States proved that it is capable of building an international system which allows nations to achieve economic success without the need for a threatening military. West Germany's security requirements were fulfilled through the multi-lateral framework of NATO with the United States shouldering the heaviest burden within the alliance. Japan's security was provided for with a bi-lateral defense treaty with the United States. By the United States taking over responsibility for defending these two nations, neighbors of Japan and Germany did not feel as threatened by a resurgence of their economic power. The ability to maintain the international system and global peace depended upon the United States to project force anywhere in the world. After entering into NATO, other security guarantees were provided outside of Europe. The Rio Pact reaffirmed the United States intention to defend the entire Western Hemisphere. The ANZUS Treaty expanded American security commitments to Australia, New Zealand and the Southwest Pacific. Bilateral treaties were signed with Taiwan and the Philippines. In 1950, the United States went to war to defend South Korea. Following the war a permanent defense treaty was signed. In 1954, the United States became party to the Southeast Asia Treaty Organization, a mutual defense pact which included Great Britain, France, Australia, New Zealand, the Philippines, Pakistan and Thailand. The security commitments the United States made to these countries continues to be a cornerstone of the international system which has prevented a resumption of great power war.

CONCLUSION

The Marshal Plan and Truman Doctrine were the
beginning of an era where the United States took
responsibility for controlling global order. As the Cold War
continued and American security commitments deepened, the
United States and the international system became one in the
same.[48] Only with American power could the international
system sustain itself against the dual challenges of rebuilding
Western Europe and Japan while at the same time containing
the Soviet Union. These policies were down payments on a
new international system which saved Western Europe from
collapse and contained Soviet power. Unfortunately, the
world divided into two international systems ideologically
opposed to one another. The liberal system would exist only
within in the confines of the United States' sphere of
influence or what would become known as the free world.
The peaceful world envisioned by Presidents Wilson,
Roosevelt and Truman could only be sustained by hardnosed
realist strategies of balancing, economic coercion and
deterrence. A single world order would not be achieved.
However, the steps taken in these crucial years helped
prevent another world war and avoided the mistakes of the

Treaty of Versailles. The foundation and the spirit of the
international system conceived during the 1940s continue
with us to the present day.

Despite the decent into what became the Cold War,
the achievements of this era were remarkable. American
policymakers constructed a liberal system based on open
economies and strong security alliances. American power
and ideas enabled a system where other nations could
prosper without resorting to force. All the world's problems
were not solved in the 1940s. In the years which followed
the world became incredibly dangerous as two superpowers,
armed with nuclear weapons, squared off against each other.
The United States did not always get the policies correct
over the course of the next 45 years. However, American
presidents never strayed too far from the fundamentals which
were established during the 1940s: containing Soviet power
and promoting free trade through open economies. By
establishing a strong philosophical foundation for what was
needed and then implementing policies to achieve those
goals, the United States not only achieved victory in the Cold
War, but proved the world does not have to exist in
perpetual conflict with itself.

CHAPTER THREE

THE AMERICAN SYSTEM WINS

The Cold War was not just an era when the United States and the Soviet Union competed for global power; it was a time when two different systems for organizing society competed over which was better suited to meet the needs of mankind. The American international system proved the superior model over its communist competitor. Unlike most international conflicts, the Cold War ended with words and votes instead of bullets and blood. The Soviet Union collapsed due to the combination of its own internal flaws and its inability to match the power of the American led international system.

Although the Soviet empire had survived for decades, by the late 1980s it could not escape the fundamental flaws inherent in communist ideology. Exorbitant oil prices during the early 1970s provided the Soviet Union with large sums of money which it spent on a massive military buildup.[1] Once oil prices dissipated in the late '70s, so too did the Soviet Union's economy. Comparatively, nations which embraced capitalism were advancing towards greater

economic integration and achieving new advancements in
computer technology.[2] These technological innovations had
a direct, positive effect on American military capabilities.[3]
Just as the Soviet Union was in decline, Ronald Reagan was
elected the fortieth President of the United States. President
Reagan rejuvenated the American military while taking a
stronger stance against Soviet aggression. He made it
abundantly clear to the Soviet Union that the United States
was both willing and able to engage in a lengthy arms race
which the Soviet Union could not possibly win.

      The inability to compete militarily with the United
States had a direct effect on East-West relations. In 1986
Mikhail Gorbachev came to power recognizing the Soviet
Union needed reform.[4] Although Gorbachev wanted to
change his country, it was not his intention for the Soviet
Union to break apart.[5] Gorbachev wanted to make internal
reforms and to improve relations with the West.[6] However,
once Gorbachev began ruination of the machine which kept
the communist party in power, events quickly engulfed the
Soviet establishment. Whereas the West was held together
through shared interests and the fact that their system
brought economic and political success, the Eastern bloc was
held together by force. Gorbachev's unwillingness to employ

force to keep order within the Soviet Union ensured that the empire which had stood for over seventy years would dissolve into the ash heap of history.

THE REAGAN ESCALATION

The Soviet empire, which stretched from the Pacific Ocean to Central Europe, from the Arctic Ocean to the borders of the Middle East, became unaffordable during the 1980s. In addition to territory directly under Moscow's control, it was supporting governments and movements in Eastern Europe, Africa and Central America. The Red Army had millions of men under arms in addition to thousands of nuclear warheads. The cost of maintaining such an empire was not cheap and only got more expensive over time. Between 1970 and 1982 the costs associated with the Soviet Union's foreign policy more than doubled.[7] These cost increases were occurring during a time of economic stagnation. According to a study by the World Bank, the Soviet Union's economic growth between 1960 and 1980 was "the worst in the world."[8] Soviet defense expenditures accounted for approximately 40 percent of the annual budget.[9] This colossal sum of money accounted for 15 to 20 percent of their GDP.[10] Additionally, overall quality of life

for the citizens of the Soviet Union only got worse. During
the mid to late 1970s, the Soviet Union made "history as the
first industrialized country to register peacetime declines in
life expectance and infant mortality."[11] In spite of these
challenges, Moscow successfully masked its problems.
During the 1970s and into the early 1980s, worldwide
communism appeared as menacing as ever.

During this time it was perceived that communist
powers were ascending while the democracies were in full
retreat. In 1975 North Vietnam dealt the United States a
humiliating defeat by conquering South Vietnam. The Soviet
Union was providing support to the Marxist governments in
Ethiopia and Angola. Communism gained appeal in Central
America. In Europe, the Soviets increased their nuclear
capability by deploying a new generation of SS-20 missiles.
In 1979, the Soviet Union took direct military action and
invaded Afghanistan.[12] This was the first time the Soviet
Union invaded a sovereign nation since World War II. In
the Middle East, Iran plunged into revolution creating an
enemy out of a major ally of the United States seemingly
overnight. The Iranians stormed the American Embassy and
paraded their hostages for the world to see. How could the
United States be a superpower if its dignity and honor could

be violated so easily? The United States appeared helpless against this onslaught. Economic problems, the political fallout from Watergate and the fact that the United States suffered the first military defeat in its history led to a sense of irreversible American decline.

After suffering defeat in Vietnam, the American military was in a poor condition and needed reform. Retired General Fred Franks Jr., who would command the U.S. 7th Corp in Operation Desert Storm, recalled that "the years of fighting in Vietnam had drawn Europe-based forces down to unacceptable strengths. Worse, the insatiable appetite for personnel stripped our forces of officer leadership, and almost destroyed the Army's professional noncommissioned officer corps, long the backbone of the Army."[13] Strategies being developed at the time were reflective of the manpower problems. Under the Active Defense doctrine of General William DePuy, the American army was being trained to defend central Europe at a three to one disadvantage.[14] A single battalion was expected to act as a covering force against six enemy battalions.[15] Although it may not have been always blatantly stated by policymakers, the conventional imbalance was to be rectified by the use of nuclear weapons. After touring NATO for the first time,

Senator Sam Nunn (D-GA) said he "became convinced that, at the battlefield front, [NATO's] military people were going to ask for nuclear release at the very beginning of any conventional war. The first reason for that was because the nuclear weapons were pretty close to the front. The second reason was that the Soviets were perceived to be much stronger with tanks and artillery and [the concern was] that we were going to have our nuclear arsenal overrun very rapidly unless it was used."[16] With such a military advantage, it is not surprising that the Soviet Union was undeterred from invading Afghanistan and supporting communist movements around the world.

Against this frightening backdrop, Ronald Reagan was elected President on a strong anti-communist platform. President Reagan, a fervent opponent of détente, believed the United States needed to take a more defiant stance against Soviet aggression. Only when the Soviet Union became less belligerent and did not oppress its people, could a true détente exist between the two superpowers. However, should such a pleasant outcome not occur, Reagan believed the United States was inherently stronger than the Soviet Union. Reagan fully understood the weakness of the Soviet system compared to that of the United States and the West.

Delivering his weekly radio address in October 1975, Reagan described the Russians and how the Cold War would inevitably proceed: "The Russian have told us over and over again their goal is to impose their incompetent and ridiculous system on the world...but what do we envision as the eventual outcome? Either they will see the fallacy of their way and give up their goal or their system will collapse or − (and we don't let ourselves think of this) we'll have to use our weapons one day."[17] Eventually, the Soviet Union both saw the flaws in their own policies and gave up their goal of spreading the workers revolution around the world. Reagan reflected in his autobiography that "the great dynamic success of capitalism had given us a powerful weapon in our battle against communism − money. The Russians could never win the arms race; we could outspend them forever."[18] As President, Reagan proved his point to the Soviet Union − it was a fruitless endeavor to compete in an arms race with the United States.

Under National Security Decision Directive (NSDD)-75, classified SECRET at the time, the United States established its formal policy for relations with the Soviet Union.[19] As NSDD-75 stated, "U.S. policy toward the Soviet Union will consist of three elements: external resistance to Soviet imperialism; internal pressure on the USSR to weaken sources of Soviet imperialism; and negotiations to eliminate, on the basis of strict reciprocity, outstanding disagreements."[20] To rectify the military situation, Reagan embarked on a massive military buildup and accelerated reform efforts already underway in the military. In 1981 the United States spent $348 billion (in 2005 dollars) on defense or 5.2% of the GDP.[21] By 1988, Reagan's last year in office, $475.5 billion was spent. Defense as an expenditure of GDP averaged 5.8% during Reagan's terms in office. Despite an increase in defense spending, on average only 23 percent of the total budget went towards national defense. Reagan was showing the Soviets that not only could the United States spend more on the military, but it could do it affordably and therefore permanently. In addition, not only would the United States spend money to defeat the Soviet Union in a conventional conflict, but it would also aid nations around the world in their own national struggles against communism.

The United States supported opposition groups around the world in an effort to roll back communist gains in third world nations. The main thrust of containing and rolling back communist advances occurred in Afghanistan.[22]

The United States provided weapons and money to the Afghan mujahedeen via Pakistan. The United States was able to make the Soviets bleed, literally. By the time the Soviet Union pulled out of Afghanistan in 1989, an estimated 15,000 Soviet military personnel had been killed and another 35,000 wounded.[23] Throughout the 1980s, the war in Afghanistan only exacerbated the Soviet Union's problems.

At a time when the Soviet Union could barely afford the arms race it was in, Reagan escalated the rhetoric against the Soviet Union and threatened to expand the arms race into space. On March 8th, 1983, before the National Organization of Evangelicals, Reagan spoke against the idea that the Cold War was a misunderstanding between two well-meaning countries. "I urge you to beware the temptation of pride – the temptation of blithely declaring yourselves above it all and label both sides equally at fault, to ignore the facts of history and the aggressive impulses of an evil empire, to simply call the arms race a giant misunderstanding and thereby remove yourself from the struggle between right and wrong and good and evil."[24] A few weeks after delivering the "evil empire" speech, Reagan addressed the nation on a new weapon system that was meant to render nuclear missiles useless. Reagan proposed a global, multi- layered missile defense system that would shoot down intercontinental ballistic missiles. The system would be a combination of missiles and space based lasers called the Strategic Defense Initiative (SDI). The technological capability of such a system did not yet exist. However, Reagan was advocating a massive scientific effort, similar to the Manhattan Project (which created the atomic bomb), towards such a goal. Critics mocked the program as "Star Wars." Although this may have come across as an idealistic fantasy to domestic opponents, the Soviets took the issue seriously.

In 1985, after the funeral of General Secretary Konstantin Chernenko, Gorbachev met with the American delegation which included Secretary of State George Schultz. Gorbachev tried to persuade the United States away from SDI by threatening that, "any new break through resulting from the scientific and technological revolution…could set in motion irreversible and uncontrollable processes."[25] Gorbachev wanted to convince the Americans that SDI would exacerbate tensions between the two superpowers. This was an attempted bluff on Gorbachev's part. He knew the Soviet Union was not in a position to compete militarily with the United States over the long term. As Robert Gates,

Director of the CIA and future Secretary of Defense described in his memoir, Soviet leaders "saw an America that apparently had the resources to increase defense spending dramatically and then add this program on top, and all of it while seeming hardly to break a sweat." SDI convinced "even some of the conservative members of the Soviet leadership that major internal changes were needed in the U.S.S.R."[26] Gorbachev was aware that as time progressed the United States military was improving its conventional capabilities while the Red Army was falling behind. For the Soviet Union, nuclear weapons increasingly became an insurance policy in the event of a conventional war. Even if a war began, it would not escalate too far because of the Soviet Union's ability to literally destroy the United States. SDI threatened this national security safety net.[27] More than fear of an actual nuclear exchange, Gorbachev and the Soviet senior leadership knew they could not afford to seriously expand the arms race into a whole new technological realm. Prior to the 1986 Reykjavik summit, Gorbachev spoke plainly to the Politburo about the difficult position the Soviet Union found itself in and the implications of SDI: "Our main goal now is to prevent the arms race from entering a new stage. If we don't do that, the danger to us will increase…We will be drawn into an arms race that we cannot manage. We will lose, because right now we are already at the end of our tether."[28] Considering the United States economy was expanding and its technology growing more sophisticated, reducing tension with the United States became necessary for the survival of the Soviet Union.

THE INTERNATIONAL SYSTEM AND THE COLD WAR

Although it was far from clear at the time, by the 1980s the seeds of the Soviet Union's demise had already been sown. The free market of the American international system allowed for the exchange of ideas and technology across national borders. Whereas nations in the American led international system became more efficient, the Soviet Union and its Warsaw Pact allies were plagued with burdening bureaucracy and economic stagnation. Reagan's policies exploited these trends allowing for an increase in overall national power compared to the Soviet Union.

Multinational corporations recognized the economic advantages of sharing technology in order to reduce cost on expensive research and development projects. As scholars

William C. Wohlforth and Stephen G. Brooks describe, "While the United States and Western Europe were able to exploit the latest technologies and production methods from throughout the world because of rapidly increasing FDI (foreign direct investment) inflows, the Soviets were largely dependent on autonomous improvements in technology and production methods."[29] These developments were taking place within new technology industries such as computers, biotechnology and communications. During the 1980s, the Soviet Union possessed only 200,000 computers, whereas the United States had twenty-five million.[30] As Wohlforth and Brooks concluded "Thus the very sectors that were becoming most internationalized in the 1980s were those that provide much of the foundation for military power in the modern era."[31] The long term outlook for the Soviet Union and communist states was one of economic and technological backwardness.

Not only were these trends understood by the United States government, but they were used to pressure the Soviet Union into making reforms. Secretary of State Shultz was keenly aware of the broad changes occurring in international economics, communications and technological development.[32] In 1986, at the request of Secretary Shultz, Foreign Service officer and intelligence analyst Richard D. Kauzlarich conducted research on what was to become known as globalization.[33] His researched showed that the costs of personal computers were becoming cheaper and that corporations were increasingly diversifying where they manufactured goods.[34] As one of Kauzlarich's memos concluded, "Increasingly, countries which cannot or will not compete in the global market place and interact with ideas from other societies will find themselves falling behind the advanced innovators and producers."[35] Shultz took these findings to the Soviet leadership in an effort to convince them that the Soviet Union had to join the West or fall irreversibly behind.[36]

Around the globe where countries found themselves divided during the Cold War, the people in the American international system were far more successful than their communist brethren. As esteemed international relations scholar Michael Mandelbaum notes, "The liberal economic order proved the more productive one. West Germany became more prosperous than East Germany, South Korea than North Korea, Taiwan than China."[37] Even poor countries of Western Europe - Ireland, Portugal, Spain and Greece grew twice as fast as communist countries in Eastern

Europe.[38] Besides economic growth, nations whose security was intertwined with the United States did not engage in major wars with other regional powers. Europe grew closer together through the European Economic Community, a precursor to the European Union. Japan expanded regional trade and acquired resources overseas from the same nations only a generation earlier it was at war with. Countries within the American sphere of influence were experiencing peace and stability. The same could not be said for countries on the other side of the East-West divide.

Not only were communist countries falling behind in terms of living standards, but personal and national security were also lacking. Communist on communist violence was not uncommon. During the Cold War states which attempted to leave the Soviet Union's sphere of influence did not fare well. In 1953 an East German rebellion against communist authorities was brutally suppressed. In 1956, Hungary attempted to leave the Warsaw Pact prompting a Soviet invasion of the country. In 1961, Premier Nikita Khrushchev erected the Berlin Wall to prevent East Berlin's best and brightest from defecting to the West. In 1968, the Czechoslovaks openly rebelled only to suffer a Soviet invasion as well. Relations between China and the Soviet

Union deteriorated from the 1950s onward. In 1969, border skirmishes between the two nations almost led to all-out war. On August 18, 1969, a Soviet diplomat inquired to a U.S. State Department Soviet Affairs specialist about how the United States would respond to a Soviet attack against China's nuclear facilities.[39] In 1978, Vietnam launched a full scale invasion of Cambodia and overthrew the Khmer Rouge. In 1979, China invaded Vietnam. Just as nations were in fear of Moscow, so was the average person in fear of their local communist security forces. Throughout the Cold War local communist apparatuses controlled the populations to ensure no dissent survived long.

While the Western world focused its attention on the Soviet Union and returning life to normal, communist nations either were forced to stay within the Soviet sphere of influence or had to fight, as China did, to free themselves. Whereas the presence of American power increased security, Soviet influence made peace more precarious and life more dangerous.

GORBACHEV AND THE END

Gorbachev set out to reform the Soviet Union but maintain the communist party in power.[40] In order to accomplish this goal, the Soviet Union had to reduce tensions with the West. Only once relations had improved could Gorbachev reduce the military's budget and overseas commitments.[41] As Gorbachev gained concessions from Reagan, he was in a better position to make reforms within the Soviet Union itself. Once Gorbachev's reforms got underway they took on a life of their own. Eastern Europe and the Soviet republics succeeded in gaining greater autonomy. Gorbachev, unlike every previous Soviet leader since Stalin, was against shedding blood in the name of class struggle. He had no intention of violently forcing people to stay within the Soviet Union. After a failed coup against Gorbachev, democratic forces throughout the Soviet empire only became stronger. One by one, the Soviet republics went their own way.

In 1986 Mikhail Gorbachev came to power after three successive elderly Soviet leaders died in office. As part of a younger generation of communists, Gorbachev had "new thinking" on how the Soviet Union had to conduct its affairs. He believed the conflict with the West was not only unnecessary but draining the economy of vital resources. As Jeff Matlock, Ambassador to the Soviet Union noted, "Once Gorbachev understood that the arms race would not be tamed nor the country's economic ills cured without opening the country to outside influence and initiating democratic reforms, the internal reform process began in earnest. Once Gorbachev started the reform process, President Reagan recognized that it was in the American interest to encourage it."[42] Gorbachev initiated reforms, however, change came slowly. Gorbachev wanted to make reforms within the state construct, not simply destroy the entire Soviet apparatus. As a result the Soviet Union became an amalgamation of capitalist and communist policies. [43] The government relaxed restrictions on the media and what could be discussed regarding government policies.[44] However, many of the same government agencies and party members who were part of the Soviet system were now given the responsibility of undoing it. This internal contradiction prevented true reform from taking place. It would not be possible for the communist party to make reforms which were contrary to the very nature of communism. At the same time, the Russian people became restless since reform was not moving fast enough. This was a recipe for disaster.

As plans began to unravel Gorbachev refused to use force to maintain order. Not only did Gorbachev refuse to use the military to keep Eastern Europe within its sphere of influence, but he also did not want to use the military to keep the Soviet Union itself held together.[45] Gorbachev began to inform Warsaw Pact countries that they could not expect assistance from the Soviet Union in the event their governments were threatened with domestic revolution. [46] In December 1988, Gorbachev gave a stirring speech before the United Nations. He renounced the Brezhnev Doctrine, which promised an invasion for any nation which attempted to leave the Soviet Union's sphere of influence. What is more, he announced that 500,000 troops would be leaving Eastern Europe. In April 1989, the communist government in Georgia requested Russian assistance to quell a protest in the capital Tbilisi. The result was the death of twenty-one Georgians. Following this incident, Gorbachev renounced force, even as a means of keeping the Soviet Union together.[47] Throughout the summer of 1989, he did nothing to keep the Eastern European communist governments in power. On November 9th 1989, the Berlin Wall came down unexpectedly. By the end of year the Warsaw Pact had virtually dissolved. In March 1990, Latvia, a republic formally part of the Soviet Union, voted to secede. Other republics followed suit. In June 1990, the Russian republic itself voted that its law trumps Union laws. The Soviet Union was coming apart.

While on vacation in the Crimea, a group of senior military and security officials unexpectedly visited Gorbachev. They demanded that he declare martial law. Gorbachev refused and he was detained. The coup lasted only three days due to the incompetence of the plotters and the charisma of Moscow Party Chief Boris Yeltsin. The failure of the coup emboldened democrats and those who wanted a complete break with communism. Although Gorbachev attempted to keep the Soviet Union together, he was unable to convince the republics and the Russian people that the Soviet Union had any virtue worth saving. On December 25th, 1991 Gorbachev was forced to resign. The following day the Soviet Union ceased to exist.

CONCLUSION

Two factors of the Cold War are relevant to the United States' present and future role in global affairs. First, the United States should always strive to have more military power than any potential adversary. The recognition by Gorbachev and others in the Soviet leadership that it was not possible to win an arms race with the United States was an essential factor in their decision to reduce tensions. Second, the international system of open economies and free trade allowed the United States and the West to advance ahead of the Soviet Union economically and technologically – the two complimenting each other.

Communism was a proven failure to those living under it before Gorbachev rose to be Premiere of the Soviet Union. The system only survived as long as it did by the threat and use of force. Once a leader came to power that was unwilling to use that force to maintain unity the entire system fell apart. Poles, Germans and even Russians themselves wanted the fruits of capitalism and democracy. As Gorbachev wrote years later, "Critics at home have also charged that we lost our allies in Eastern Europe, that we surrendered these countries without compensation…The system that existed in Eastern and Central Europe was condemned by history, as was the system in our own country…Moreover, this system could have been 'saved' in only one way – by sending in tanks, as we did in Czechoslovakia in 1968. The consequences of such unjustified action could have included a general European war."[48] By removing force as a means of persuasion, the Soviet empire dissolved.

The size and efficiency of the United States' economy guaranteed a superior amount of military power compared to the Soviet Union. However, even with such power, the Soviet Union still posed a threat to the United States. It supported Marxist movements around the world and possessed enough nuclear weapons to destroy the United States. Additionally, when the United States did not devout the necessary resources to defense and when the military was suffering due to the effects of the Vietnam War, the Soviet Union became a much larger threat than at any time since the start of the Cold War. By the late 1970s and even into the early 1980s it was certainly conceivable that the United States and NATO would have lost a conventional conflict with the Soviet Union. Fortunately, debate over what an actual war between the two super powers would have looked like will forever stay within the realm of academic discussion. However, in the future it is entirely possible that through a global shift in economic power, poor policy choices by the United States or both, other nations could develop military capabilities which could challenge American interests regionally and even globally.

The Western democracies stayed allied based on a mutual shared interest in defending themselves against the Soviet Union and communism. Whereas wars constantly broke out between communist nations, Western democracies disagreed on policy, but would never even contemplate open war against each other. As the Berlin Wall came down and history marched steadily away from the Cold War, the global position of the United States expanded. Absent the unifying threat, numerous scholars and experts expected the United States' influence to wane. Essentially, its large military presence throughout the globe would no longer be needed. Yet, this did not occur. In fact, the United States military continued to be welcomed in Europe, the Middle East and East Asia. The question is why.

CHAPTER FOUR

THE AMERICAN SYSTEM SPREADS

After the collapse of the Soviet Union, the United States had an unprecedented amount of power compared to any other nation.[1] Its power was so preponderant that no other nation or group of nations could pose any serious challenge to American influence. Historian Paul Kennedy left no doubt about this historic precedence in an opinion piece in the Financial Times: "Nothing has ever existed like this disparity of power; nothing. I have returned to all of the comparative defense spending and military personnel statistics over the past 500 years that I compiled in *Rise and Fall of the Great Powers*, and no other nation comes close."[2] Given such a large power disparity and the fear this would instill in other nations, there was a school of thought which said nations would ally together to balance against the United States.[3] However, this never occurred. In fact, more than twenty years after the collapse of the Soviet Union, alliances forged during the early days of the Cold War continue.

During the 1990s the United States leveraged its power to expand and consolidate the international system it created in the 1940s. In search of a grand strategy to guide the United States in a world without the Soviet Union, the Department of Defense produced a memo called the Defense Planning Guidance. Although this document is produced every two years to help establish budget priorities, 1992 was the first time it was produced since the Cold War ended. Thus, it took on greater meaning than previous editions. The Defense Planning Guidance was written principally by Zalmay Khalizad, but reflected the thinking of Paul Wolfowitz, Lewis Scooter Libby, Stephen Hadley, Eric Eldelmen and Dick Cheney.[+] All would go on to have important positions in the George W. Bush Administration and be labeled "neo-conservatives", more often than not in a derogatory manner. In March 1992, a draft of the Defense Planning Guidance leaked to the media. This seminal report declared that, "Our first objective is to prevent the re-emergence of a new rival. This is a dominant consideration underlying the new regional defense strategy and requires that we endeavor to prevent any hostile power from dominating a region whose resources would, under consolidated control, be sufficient to generate global power.

These regions include Western Europe, East Asia, the territory of the former Soviet Union and Southwest Asia."[5] The strategy being outlined was meant to permanently avoid another great power conflict and keep the United States the dominant force in global politics.

The leaked draft of the Defense Planning Guidance sparked controversy not just for its bellicose tone, but because it talked about current allies, such as Germany and Japan, as potential future aggressors. Criticism came from across the political spectrum. Bill Clinton's campaign aide George Stephanopoulos remarked that it was "one more attempt to find an excuse for big budgets instead of downsizing."[6] President George H.W. Bush's National Security Advisor, General Brent Scowcroft, called the paper "nutty."[7] Senator Joseph Biden said it was wrong for the Pentagon to construct a "Pax Americana, a global security system where threats to stability are suppressed or destroyed by U.S. military power."[8] Despite the attacks on the document, over the next twenty years this is precisely the policy which was followed by Presidents Bill Clinton and George W. Bush. After the collapse of the Soviet Union the international system continued to expand. The United States contained, reduced or eliminated threats before they could pose the same danger as the now extinct Soviet Union. The result has been over two decades of peaceful coexistence amongst the leading powers of the world.

POWER TO KEEP THE PEACE

In the late 1980s and the early 1990s, it was conceivable that having achieved economic power, Germany, Japan or a united Europe would challenge the American designed security structure in their respective regions.[9] Of course this did not occur. Even after more than 20 years since the Cold War, the United States military continues to be welcomed on German and Japanese soil, as well as other countries around the world. Why would countries, which have enough economic power to construct militaries suitable for their own defense continue to allow foreign militaries into their country? First, security was already being provided by the United States. The United States committed itself towards the defense of Europe, East Asia and eventually the Middle East during the Cold War with successful results. As was described in the previous chapter war between nations within the American sphere of influence did not occur. Second, the continued American military presence reassured the neighbors of Germany and Japan that these nations

would not seek security unilaterally outside of the U.S.-
European and U.S.-Japanese defense structure.[10] During the
1990s and even to a small extent in our present time, there is
fear that revived German and Japanese military power could
once again plunge their regions into war. As President
Clinton's Secretary of State Warren Christopher explained,
"While the tensions of the Cold War have subsided, many
Asian nations harbor apprehensions about their closest
neighbors. An American withdrawal would magnify those
concerns. And so America must stay engaged."[11] The far
reaching and superior military capability of the United States
stabilizes the international system.

    The distinctive factor which separates the United
States military from all other militaries is its ability to
"command the commons."[12] Only the United States is able to
project power on a global level. While other countries are
capable of using force within their own regions, no other
nation can use force far from its own shores to the extent the
United States is able to. At sea, in the air and in space the
United States is the dominant force. The United States'
ability to project such force is the underlying base of the
entire international system. As scholar Barry Posen
describes "Command of the commons is the key military

enabler of the U.S. global power position...Command of the commons also helps the United States to weaken its adversaries, by restricting their access to economic, military, and political assistance."[13] The inability of other states to contest the American military in the commons means to a certain extent nations need to rely upon the benevolence and good sense of the United States not to abuse its position as "commander" of the sea, air and space. The unmatched military power is a central reason why the international system, protected by the United States, was rarely challenged following the end of the Cold War.

EUROPE

Under Presidents Bill Clinton and George W. Bush, NATO increased its membership and adjusted itself for 21st century threats. NATO expanded from sixteen members at the end of the Cold War to twenty eight members as of 2011. NATO continues to reassure allies against Germany and hedges against any future revived Russian aggressor. Although the idea of Russia or Germany starting a war seems far-fetched, nations are not going to change the core tenants of a security arrangement which has avoided great power conflict on a continent whose entire history is written in blood.

Following the end of the Cold War, it was conceivable that the United States would remove its military forces from Europe and great power politics would return to the continent.[14] Others thought that Europe would increasingly evolve into a single country and challenge the United States on international issues.[15] However, these events did not occur. The United States continues to keep over eighty thousand troops in Europe.[16] In the 1990s, NATO expanded into Eastern Europe, including republics formerly part of the Soviet Union. President Clinton brought new members into NATO not just for military reasons, but as a means of spreading the fruits of democracy and capitalism to Eastern Europe. The idea was that the quicker Cold War divisions between East and West faded the better.[17] NATO's first Secretary General, Lord Hastings Ismay, believed the purpose of the alliance was to "keep the Americans in, the Russians out, and the Germans down."[18] In many ways, these three goals continue to this day.

Deep inside many pacified, integration loving, defense-expenditure-cutting Europeans is the memory of what Europe once was and could become again: realpolitik, mechanized for war; and horrifically efficient at killing en masse. When Germany reunified in 1989 there was hardly a consensus on the matter.[19] Reflecting on the momentous decision to accept the reunification of Germany former British Prime Minister Margaret Thatcher wrote, "But nor could I then or now regard Germany as just another country whose future was a matter for Germans alone to decide, without involving anybody else. A united Germany was bound to become once again the dominant power in Europe. It would...be culpably naïve, to ignore the fact that this German drive for dominance has lead in my lifetime to two terrible, global wars during which nearly a hundred million people – including of course nine million Germans – died."[20] Indeed, when Secretary of Defense Donald Rumsfeld discussed a global realignment of U.S. forces, Western Europe shuddered at the idea of modifying the number of troops in Europe.[21] NATO brings everyone into the same security umbrella and thus security decisions for the continent are made collectively as opposed to unilaterally. This fact reduces fear within member states about each other's intentions. The American military presence also provides an incentive for nations to avoid spending copious sums of money on their own militaries. Within NATO, other than the United States no nation spends even 3 percent of their GDP on defense.[22] European nations' small militaries which lack serious offensive capabilities have reduced tensions on the continent. However, the lack of capabilities combined with a violent history also makes them nervous about a departure of American forces.

Europe will continue to fear a revived Russian power bent on reclaiming its influence over the lost territories which made up the Soviet Union. Since the end of the Cold War, Russia has invaded Georgia, meddled in the affairs of the Ukraine, launched a cyber-attack against Estonia and used its oil and gas reserves as economic weapons. Absent the American security guarantees, other nations would have a need to increase their military capabilities. Given Russia's nuclear arsenal, it is probable that other nations would attempt to develop their own nuclear armaments in an effort to deter Russian aggression.[23] Such acts would not only have consequences for Europe's relationship with Russia, but would also cause severe crises within Europe itself. It would just be a matter of time before the United States would return to Europe, possibly for another continental war. While the United States established a strong security structure for Europe, the future of East Asia is far more uncertain.

EAST ASIA

All American policies and relationships within East Asia are now China-centric. The United States presence in the Pacific, much like Europe, reassured nations that Japan would not feel the need to seek security unilaterally while at the same time hedging against future threats.[24] However, unlike Europe, there is a clear challenge to regional security. China's economic power has increased dramatically since it opened its economy. The rise of a hostile China would be far more destabilizing and challenging for international security that a resurgent Germany or Russia. While Germany and Russia are potential regional challengers, the sheer size of China's population, probable economic power and present military capabilities make it a current regional power with the potential to challenge American power globally.

For over twenty years the United States under different Presidents has practiced a policy of "congagement."[25] Congagement is partly containment against any potential military aggression or political acts which are detrimental to American interests. However, it is also part engagement. The United States wants China to keep embracing capitalism with the idea that it will eventually lead China to democratize and become a responsible stakeholder in the international system. This policy is reflective of the United States' decision to support Taiwan while at the same time increasing trade with China.

In 1995, China was suspicious that Taiwan's President Lee Teng-hui was attempting to build a platform for the official independence of Taiwan. Gaining international recognition as a sovereign state is a means of achieving this goal. In June 1995, President Lee Teng-hui was allowed to speak at his alma-mater, Cornell University. In response, China's ambassador left the United States as a form of diplomatic retaliation.[26] Shortly thereafter, China fired missiles around Taiwan as means of intimidation. The following year China began amassing troops in the providence opposite Taiwan and announced live fire drills in the strait. In response the United States amassed the largest fleet in the South Pacific since the Vietnam War. China effectively backed down and ended its military exercises early.[27] Throughout the Bush Administration, the United States continued its policy of defending Taiwan by selling sophisticated arms packages to the island to China's chagrin.

At the same time, through economic engagement the United States hoped to modify China's behavior, making it more open, transparent and reflective of Western values. China has made strides in opening its economy, however, politically it still remains a repressive regime. The Chinese Communist Party's (CCP) dictatorial impulses were on display when the government ordered the murder of protesters at Tiananmen Square in 1989. Although the Sino-U.S. relationship did not return to the pre-Nixon days of diplomatic isolation, the Tiananmen Square massacre set back China's relationship with the United States. Through trade President Clinton tried to move the Sino-U.S. relationship beyond Tiananmen. After extensive negotiations with the United States, China was granted Permanent Normal Trade Relationship (PNTR) status. Under PNTR China allowed unrestrictive distribution rights for foreign companies in China and the United States gradually reduced tariffs on Chinese products. These reforms were also part of China's eventual acceptance in the World Trade Organization in 2000.[28] Despite the close economic bonds between the United States and China, the two nations disagree on a host of international issues such as American military intervention for virtually any purpose and the virtues of democracy. However, the most pressing concern for the United States and countries across Asia is how China will act while its power increases.

As East Asia's economy becomes increasingly reliant upon China, regional leaders are worried over how China will use this leverage. Jong-Wha Lee, the chief economist for the Asian Development Bank, opined, "Not just the size, but the speed of China's emerging power is really unprecedented in the region. So it creates a lot of issues — not just trade and exchange-rate policies. But in the future, what will be the role of China?"[29] Lee's words echo the concerns of millions across Asia and the world as well. China's territorial disputes with India, claims over disputed islands in the South China Sea (the Spratley Islands), and its military exercises close to Japanese waters make China's neighbors wary of Beigjing's regional goals. As a result, the United States continues to be welcomed in the region from traditional allies such as Japan, South Korea and Australia, as well as its one-time enemy, Vietnam. Fortunately, even in lieu of these difficulties, peace still reigns across East Asia.

While the 1990s and the 2000s drew concerns over the future role of China in East Asia's security structure, it was in the Middle East where the United States was called upon to wage war in defense of regional security and the international system.

THE MIDDLE EAST

Do to the heavy reliance of the global economy on oil, maintaining peace in this region is necessary and burdensome. Under the American led international system geo-politics has limited influence on the price of oil. While political instability within the region does cause price fluctuations, nations do not often use oil as a political weapon. For example, when the United States has a political dispute with China, the American government does not pressure the Saudi government in Riyadh to stop selling oil to the Chinese. As another example, President Hugo Chavez of Venezuela may deride American imperialism but that does not stop him from selling the precious commodity to American consumers. Under the American international system oil trades take place in a single global market, thus who controls the oil does not have a significant impact on its price. Oil, like any other commodity, is not an end in and of itself. It is a means towards acquiring wealth. Once a nation acquires wealth it can use that wealth as its government sees fit. Most nations are content with the current global oil market since it limits political competition over who controls oil while giving every nation the opportunity of acquiring enough wealth to meet the needs of its citizens. Of course, life does not always run so smoothly. When Iraq invaded Kuwait in August 1990, it embarked on an adventure not just to conquer Kuwait but to use oil as a means of undoing the entire balance of power in the Middle East.

In the waning days of the Cold War, Iraq became the focus of American interests in the region. Iraq's invasion of Kuwait in 1990 posed a direct challenge to the global order the United States had built and sought to expand. If Iraq had gained control of Kuwait, Saddam Hussein could have used his increased wealth to construct a formidable military designed to expand Iraq's power throughout the Middle East. Iraq would have been in a position to manipulate the oil market to its own advantage, shifting the regional balance of power in Iraq's favor to the detriment of not just American interests but the entire peaceful global order the United States was constructing. After Iraq's expulsion from Kuwait, Saddam continued to threaten American interests and seek weapons of mass destruction (WMD). The United States showed a willingness to spend an enormous amount of blood and treasure to ensure Saddam never achieved his goals.

Fear of a single power dominating the Middle East first became acute when the Soviet Union invaded Afghanistan in 1979. In President Jimmy Carter's 1980 State of the Union address, Carter warned the American public that "The Soviet Union is now attempting to consolidate a strategic position, therefore, that poses a grave threat to the free movement of Middle East oil…it demands collective efforts to meet this new threat to security in the Persian Gulf and in Southwest Asia."[30] Carter then put the Soviet Union on notice saying, "Let our position be absolutely clear: An attempt by any outside force to gain control of the Persian Gulf region will be regarded as an assault on the vital interests of the United States of America, and such an assault will be repelled by any means necessary, including military force."[31] The fear of a Soviet attack on the Persian Gulf was lifted after the superpower was defeated in Afghanistan. However, American interests in the region remained.

In 1991 those interests were threatened when Iraq invaded and occupied Kuwait. Combined, Iraq and Kuwait make up 20% of the world's oil reserves.[32] With this newly acquired wealth, Iraq would have been in a position to challenge American power in the region and posture itself for the possible conquest of its other neighbors. Prior to the invasion, Saddam was accusing Kuwait of stealing oil from the Rumailla field, which was located in both Iraq and Kuwait. Saddam demanded $2.4 billion from Kuwait as a compensation for their theft.[33] Had the invasion of Kuwait been accepted by the international community more demands and violence would have followed against other countries. By liberating Kuwait, the United States showed its willingness to risk a high number of casualties in defense of regional security. Special Assistant to President George H.W. Bush, Richard N. Haass, described the game changing nature of Saddam's acquisition of Kuwait: "An Iraq in possession of all of Kuwait's financial and mineral resources would have become not just *a* but *the* dominant local power."[34] The oil revenue would have translated into increased military capability. As Haass asserts, "Iraq, we now know, also would have gained nuclear weapons within years."[35] Bush was able to organize a coalition to liberate Kuwait because the balance of power within the Middle East was at stake and the fundamentals of the international system were being challenged. Despite suffering a humiliating defeat in the Persian Gulf War, Saddam Hussein remained in power. Over the course of the next twelve years, the United States attempted to contain Saddam.

Military confrontation between Iraq and the United States was constant throughout the 1990s. In January 1993, coalition forces attacked Iraqi air defense systems. Shortly thereafter cruise missiles targeted a factory which was part of Saddam's nuclear program.[36] In June of 1993, President Clinton ordered a cruise missile strike against Iraqi intelligence headquarters in response to an assassination attempt against former President George Bush. In 1994, Saddam tried to coerce the U.N. into lifting sanctions against Iraq by deploying 80,000 troops near the border with Kuwait. In response, Clinton ordered 50,000 troops to the region. After the crisis faded, the United States had 20,000 troops permanently stationed around Iraq to enforce the No Fly Zone and to respond to any aggressive acts.[37] In 1996, the Iraqi military attacked Kurdish towns in violation of a U.N Security Council Resolution. Once again, cruise missiles were launched in retaliation. These low level retaliatory attacks appeared to have no effect on Saddam's ability to control Iraq and defy the international community. A growing number of people in and out of government began to contemplate and advocate for stronger action again Saddam's regime.[38]

In 1998, Clinton signed the Iraq Liberation Act, which made regime change in Iraq the official policy of the United States and authorized close to $100 million in support of democratic opposition groups.[39] At the forefront in the minds of policy makers was Saddam's desire to obtain weapons of mass destruction. He had used these weapons against Iran in the 1980s as well as against his own people to suppress rebellions. After U.N. weapons inspectors were kicked out of the country in 1998, Clinton launched the most sustained bombardment of Iraq since the Persian Gulf War - Operation Desert Fox. Over a four day period, the United States and the United Kingdom launched over six hundred sorties against one hundred targets in Iraq.[40] President Clinton justified this action by stating Saddam's intention to develop and *use* WMD. In a speech from the Oval Office, Clinton warned the American people that, "if Saddam can cripple the weapons inspections system and get away with it, he would conclude that the international community, led by the United States, has simply lost its will. He will surmise that he has free rein to rebuild his arsenal of destruction. And some day, make no mistake, he will use it again, as he has in the past."[41] In case the viewer didn't get the point the first time, near the end of the speech Clinton repeated the focus of his message that Saddam was a threat and will use WMD if he is able to obtain them: "And mark my words, he will develop weapons of mass destruction. He will deploy them, and he will use them."[42] At the time the mission was seen as a complete success by the Clinton Administration. However, Saddam remained in power and it was unclear how much of an effect airstrikes actually had on Saddam's WMD programs.

During President George W. Bush's early days in office, the coalition which maintained economic sanctions against Saddam began to break apart. Not only did France, Germany and Russia have economic interests in ending the sanctions, but these same sanctions placed a burden on the average Iraqi citizen while doing little to weaken Saddam's hold over the country. After the September 11th 2001 terrorist attacks, a sense of urgency filled the Bush Administration. As Bush recalled "Before 9/11, Saddam was a problem America might have been able to manage…The lesson of 9/11 was that if we waited for a danger to fully materialize, we would have waited too long."[43] Bush feared that Saddam would develop WMD to blackmail the international community and possibly give them to terrorist groups. Secretary of Defense Donald Rumsfeld's views on Iraq went beyond Saddam's links with "terrorism" and his "genocidal acts."[44] Rumsfeld recognized that "previous attempts to reduce the risks Saddam posed had failed."[45] Saddam had regional ambitions and U.S. policy was not deterring him.[46]

Although U.N. weapons inspectors returned to Iraq in November 2002, they could not say definitively the state of Iraq's WMD program. Others such as Deputy Executive Chairman of U.N. Special Commission Charles Duelfer did not believe the U.N. mission could succeed, comparing it to inspection regimes of Germany during the interwar years.[47] In addition, the intelligence community had a history of underestimating or completely missing other countries' nuclear weapons programs. The intelligence community failed to discover India's nuclear weapons program.[48] On the very same subject, Iraq, the intelligence community did not realize how far along Iraq's nuclear weapons program was prior to Operation Desert Storm.[49] Although the CIA as well as intelligence agencies of the United States' allies believed Saddam had a WMD program, how far it had developed was unclear.

The United States faced a difficult choice over how to handle the Iraq problem. Unlike the previous Gulf War, which restored the normal balance of power; this new war with Iraq would dramatically change the status quo. At the heart of the policy debate over the second Iraq war was whether or not the United States should violate a core pillar of the international system – national sovereignty. Had Iraq successfully developed nuclear weapons, the entire balance of power in the Middle East would have been undone, possibly leading other nations to develop nuclear weapons of their own. Nuclear weapons are a cheap means towards military parity. If Iraq had developed nuclear weapons, Saddam would be able to deter any conventional attacks against Iraq. Nations would be wary that even a small conflict with Iraq could quickly escalate beyond anyone's control. In addition, just as Western leaders now worry about Pakistan's nuclear arsenal falling into the hands of Islamic terrorists, those concerns would also apply to a nuclear armed Iraq.

Given the recent failure of the intelligence community to predict the 9/11 attacks, combined with Saddam's history of aggression, the Bush Administration concluded that only regime change could solve the Iraq problem. Despite the initial success of the invasion, the

United States became bogged down in Iraq due to an insurgency by regime loyalists and Al-Qaeda terrorists. The United States did not find large quantities of weapons of mass destruction, undermining a core justification for the war. During Saddam's Federal Bureau of Investigation (FBI) interrogation, Saddam revealed that he wanted Iran to think he had weapons of mass destruction as a means of deterrence.[50] In addition, he stated his intentions to acquire weapons of mass destruction.[51] The United States eventually stabilized the country and presided over democratic elections. However, even after the United States withdrew from Iraq, the American military still maintains a force of 20,000 troops in the region to deal with any potential threats.[52] The Iraq war will surely be debated for years to come. It should be noted that for all the heartache, mistakes and problems with Operation Iraqi Freedom, the result was a totally defeated Iraq. This is not to say that policymakers should look to Iraq as a model on how to conduct foreign policy. The strategic goal was sound, but the tactics used to achieve that goal were severely flawed. Nevertheless, the Saddam regime is gone and Iraq is neither in a position nor has the intention of attacking its neighbors. The balance of power in the Middle East remains favorable to American interests.

CONCLUSION

An outcome of the great power wars during the 20th century (the two world wars and the Cold war), was that the United States prevented any one nation from dominating the major economic centers of the world. If any nation gained total control over Europe, the Middle East or East Asia the world would be a much more dangerous place for the United States. After the Cold War, the United States kept its military forward deployed in places far from North America to deal with small threats before they became large ones. In addition, American troops reassured the United States' allies that the security structure of the previous decades would remain intact. This policy has resulted in lengthy peace between the major powers of the world. Although conflict still occurs, such as in the Balkans or in the Middle East, great power war did not return following the collapse of the Soviet Union. The "Pax Americana" system derided by Senator Biden has avoided a return to the multi-polar balance of power politics which led to so many wars throughout European history. The United States had achieved a preponderance of power so great that other nations either could not or would not dare to balance against it. Those nations that did try to confront the United States, like Iraq, did not fare well. Similar to any mechanical system, the international system constructed by the United States needs constant upgrades, modifications and maintenance if it is going to last year after year. Unfortunately, through poor policy decisions the United States is embarking on a course detrimental to its own interests and the stability of the international system it worked so hard to construct.

False arguments of "imperial overstretch" combined with the real economic and financial crisis are causing many to argue the United States needs to cut defense spending, reduce its security commitments and return to a "normal" foreign policy.[53] These arguments sound soothing to the ears of war weary citizens whose responsibilities appear never ending and rewards never coming. However, going down such a path will usher in conflicts the United States would otherwise be able to avoid. Given its current challenges, the question is how should the United States act in the world to achieve the same peaceful environment which has benefited so many around the globe?

CHAPTER FIVE

THE ONCE AND FUTURE GUARDIAN

Nations have made enormous progress this past century in terms of how they interact with one another. During the first half of the 20th century competition between powerful nations ultimately led to global war. Following these conflicts, the two remaining superpowers had different visions of how the world should be structured – the American vision won. During the 1990s and into the 2000s, a core assumption of the international system was that the United States was powerful enough to influence, deter and if necessary defeat any nation which threatened the system. In addition, it was assumed that free markets would be universally adopted and the economic prosperity produced would satisfy the demands of governments and citizens alike. Both those assumptions have now been called into question.

There is a growing belief that the United States is unable to continue to be the guardian of the international system. The argument at first glance appears strong: egregious levels of spending have plunged the nation into historic levels of debt; ten years of war with international terrorism, including heavy fighting in Iraq and Afghanistan, has left the military exhausted. The ongoing financial crisis threatens globalization and the ability of countries to maintain open economies. In 2007, billionaire Steve Forbes confidently declared that, "This is the richest year in human history. The best way to create wealth is to have free markets and free people, and more and more of the world is realizing it."[1] The following year the entire financial industry was on the verge of collapse and with it the American economy. To make matters more difficult, emerging economies are increasingly accounting for a greater share of the world's wealth, which suggests that over time their power will increase to the detriment of American influence. Given this new reality, many believe that the United States should retrench – reduce its security commitments and begin to act more "normal" in international affairs.[2] Some within this line of thought believe the decline of American power is inevitable, which is all the more reason the United States should take action now before events reduce the country's options.[3]

Although the financial crisis and the subsequent debt burden do pose a real danger to the United States' position in the world, acting on the belief that the United States has irretrievably lost influence can make arguments about decline a self-fulfilling prophecy. The United States still has the power to meet its security commitments and thus continue to be the prime guardian of the international system. Not only does the United States still have enough power, but the openness of the global economy has held up remarkably well in the face of a severe recession. Following the financial crisis nations did not turn inward as they did during the 1930s. At the 2009 G-20 summit in London leaders of the most prosperous nations assured the world that, "We will not repeat the historic mistakes of protectionism of previous eras."[+] Somewhere in the heavens, John Maynard Keynes, Cordell Hull and the rest of the architects of Bretton Woods were smiling. The spirit of Bretton Woods has endured, at least for now.

This is not to say there are no threats to the American led international system. The genius of international trade under the American system is that nations can succeed without causing others to fail. This has been a significant factor of the enduring peace between great powers. However, increased government intervention in the markets will give an unfair advantage to certain nations at the expense of others. Those nations who feel cheated will respond with their own government measures such as tariffs on goods, import quotas or whatever other means are at their disposal. As the Chief Foreign Affairs commentator for the Financial Times described, the world is in danger of moving from a "win-win" world, to a "zero-sum" world.[5] The financial crisis reinforced perceptions in Beijing, Moscow and even Washington D.C. that governments must play a more active role in markets. Government intervention in the markets is typically used to achieve political stability, not economic efficiency. As a result market intervention by governments has the potential to undermine the open nature of the global economy and cause economic conflict between nations.

The two nations which have the most potential to find themselves at odds with one another are China and the United States. As the two largest economies in the world, the relationship between the United States and China will have a significant impact on the international system. Unlike other emerging powers, China is constructing a military designed to prevent American forces from intervening militarily in East Asia. Already China's improved military capabilities has forced the United States military to rethink how it would fight a naval and air war in the region.[6] China's appetite for influence will continue to grow in tandem with its power. These developments pose the greatest danger to the international system since the Cold War days of the Soviet Union.

DEFICITS, DEBT AND DECLINE

While some arguments over the decline of American power are exaggerated, the dangers posed by fiscal imbalances facing the Unite States are all too real. If the United States does not figure out a way to reform its entitlement system so that it is both affordable and provides a satisfactory level of care the United States will be unable to fulfill its security commitments.

In an effort to minimize the effects of the 2008 financial crisis the United States bought portions of the country's largest banks at the cost of $470 billion.[7] This was followed by a stimulus package costing approximately $800 billion. These measures were designed to prevent financial calamity and jumpstart the economy. The only way to spend such staggering amounts of money is by running a budget deficit. At the end of 2008, the deficit stood at $458.5 billion. By the end of 2009, this number had jumped $1.4 trillion. The deficit to GDP ratio had reached 10 percent, the highest level since 1945.[8] Although financial calamity was averted, strong economic growth did not return. While the recession officially ended in June 2009, the economy continues to stagnate with low levels of economic growth.[9] Through the first three quarters of 2011 the economy only grew on average a little over 1 percent.[10] This is abysmally low, especially coming out of a recession which usually sees high growth rates. With each passing year, low growth exacerbates the country's debt problem. As of 2011, the total debt surpassed $15 trillion. Even with low interest rates, this amount of debt is difficult to manage. In the near future mounting debt will wreck the American economy. In addition, weak consumer spending by American citizens will be a drag on the world economy causing further economic and political uncertainty around the world. Without a strong economic base, the United States cannot afford a military capable of projecting the necessary power to maintain the international system.

The economic crisis accelerated existing trends in government spending hastening the day the United States meets financial ruin. In the coming years entitlement spending will cause the nation's debt to become unsustainable. In 1962 mandatory entitlement spending represented approximately 26 percent of the federal budget.[11] By 2011, entitlement spending grew to over 56 percent of all federal spending. According to the National Commission for Fiscal Responsibility and Reform, established by President Barack Obama, by 2025 all government revenue will be consumed by interest payments, Medicare, Medicaid and Social Security.[12] The rest of the government will be financed by taking on even more debt. According to the Congressional Budget Office (CBO), by 2035 spending on mandatory health care programs alone will consume 10 percent of the GDP.[13] By this point the debt will already be 185 percent of the GDP.[14] Inevitably interest rates will rise, reducing lending, making it more difficult for new companies to establish themselves, existing companies to hire and ultimately reducing U.S. GDP.[15] Understanding that it is entitlement spending which makes the debt unsustainable is essential to formulating the correct policy to deal with the fiscal crisis.

A false argument is that the wars in Iraq and Afghanistan are a primary cause of the United States' fiscal challenges. If this were the case, long term projections for the debt would not be as daunting considering the United States is now out of Iraq and plans to exit Afghanistan as well. Even if the wars in *both* Iraq and Afghanistan did not occur, the United States would still have a crippling debt problem. As of the spring 2011, the United States had spent approximately $1.3 trillion on the wars in Iraq and Afghanistan. This also includes non-Department of Defense related appropriations such as funding for the State Department/USAID, diplomatic operations and healthcare costs for wounded veterans.[16] Breaking down these numbers further $806 billion went towards Iraq and $444 billion went towards Afghanistan.[17] This is certainly huge sums of money. But to say it is a structural cause of the debt is misleading. If the United States did not engage in Operation Enduring Freedom and Operation Iraqi Freedom the country would still be facing a debt crisis at the same level of severity.

The current level of defense spending is actually at an historic low.[18] During the Cold War, the United States spent on average of about 7.5 percent of the GDP on defense. Comparatively, from 2002 to 2011, the average percentage of the GDP spent on defense was around 4 percent. This number is projected to fall to about 3.5 percent by 2016. As a percentage of all outlays for the federal budget, defense spending accounted for an average of 40 percent during the Cold War. After 1974, defense spending as a portion of the budget fell below 30 percent until the Soviet Union disintegrated. Again, far more was spent on defense during the Cold War compared to the current conflicts in Afghanistan and Iraq. From 2002 to 2011, the United States annual budget outlays for defense have been just under 20 percent. Under the President's 2013 budget, this number is projected to fall to 12.5 percent by 2017. The stubborn truth of numbers reveals that reducing defense spending does nothing to ameliorate the country's fiscal problems. The only thing these reductions will accomplish is to weaken American military capabilities and tempt aggressors to challenge American primacy in their regions.

Defense budget cuts are occurring at a time when other countries need the United States to reassure them that the international system is durable and will continue to survive over the long term. The global economic crisis is still ongoing with Europe in turmoil and the possibility that China's economy is slowing down. During a time of economic uncertainty, as the only global superpower the United States must have the capability to reassure nations that security arrangements within their regions will not be altered. Economic uncertainty can quickly have unforeseen political consequences. Considering the United States military underpins security in the leading economic regions of the world, it is folly to undermine that foundation at a time when the future is opaque. It is possible that rising economic powers will take advantage of the economic difficulties currently plaguing the United States and seek to alter the international system to better suit their interests.

SUCCESS OF THE OTHERS

The rise of new economic powers may cause a relative loss of American economic influence over the long term; however most of these nations will not be able to build militaries capable of challenging American power in their regions. As a result, even in a multi-polar economic world the United States will still be in a position to maintain security in areas vital to its interests. Nevertheless, the rise of new economic powers is still an historic event. The comprehensive report *Global Trends 2025,* published by the United States Intelligence Community in 2008, is crystal clear, "In terms of size, speed, and directional flow, the global shift in relative wealth and economic power now under way—roughly from West to East—is without precedent in modern history."[19] As the economist Roger Gilpin describes, typically rising powers try to remake the world in their own image by changing "the rules governing the international system, the division of the spheres of influence, and most important of all, the international distribution of territory."[20] In order to handle the economic transition underway the level of danger posed by rising nations must be adequately appreciated while at the same time not be overhyped.

In the coming decades, economies currently understood to be still developing will be larger than the world's current largest economies. In 2003, Goldman Sachs coined the term "BRICs", to describe the emerging economies of Brazil, Russia, India and China. Goldman Sachs argued that by 2050, these nations would collectively constitute the largest economies in the world.[21] PricewaterhouseCoopers followed up with their own idiom, the "E7", in reference to the seven largest emerging economies (the Brazil, India, Russia, China plus Turkey, Indonesia and Mexico).[22] In 2000, the combined GDP of the United States, the United Kingdom, Canada, France, Italy, Germany and Japan (G-7) was more than twice that of the E-7. According to PricewaterhouseCoopers, this will change over time. By 2019 the E-7 and G-7's GDP will be nearly identical. By 2030 the E-7's total GDP will be about 30 percent higher than the GDP of the G-7.[23] To rearticulate, by 2030 collective emerging economies will be greater than the current largest economies. As was previously discussed, there is a fear that these rising economic powers will seek to alter the international system to better suit their interests.

Fortunately, only nations which are capable of converting their wealth into military power pose a danger to the United States and the international system. Economic changes are a far cry from bringing forth, or being able to bring forth, political changes to international security. As historian Paul Kennedy reminded us, there is significant lag time between when a nation becomes an economic power and when it can become a military power.[24] Indeed, this time may never come, as there are many other variables at play, such as population, size and geography. No one worries about an invasion from Singapore. That being said nations which are not equipped to challenge the United States may try anyway.

Turkey and Brazil unsuccessfully attempted to influence the international response to Iran's nuclear program. In May of 2010 Turkey and Brazil announced a deal that was struck with Iran over its enriched uranium.[25] Brazil and Turkey made an offer to have Iran's low enriched uranium shipped out of the country and converted into fuel for a nuclear reactor. The Obama Administration rejected the deal and it went nowhere.[26] Brazil and Turkey probably do not want to see Iran acquire nuclear weapons. Rather, they saw an opportunity to have a say on world events and they took it. Beyond gaining a high degree of media attention and reigniting discussion over the changing geopolitical landscape, Brazil and Turkey failed to alter regional security dynamics in any meaningful way. The two countries economic power does not translate into political influence. The United States or any nation which can unilaterally alter another nation's security for good or ill will always have more influence than a nation or group of nations which lack such a capability. This metric is not based upon any region's particular culture or diplomatic preference, but rather it is simply the unforgiving nature of international politics.

Given that force will always be the ultimate arbiter of international disputes, the United States must be wary of any nation which increases its military power to alter regional security. Thus far, China and India have made efforts to increase their military capabilities. However, India continues to face threats internally from Islamic terrorism, to the west its historic enemy Pakistan and to the northeast it must hedge against a potentially hostile China. These constraining factors reduce the threat posed by India's increased military capability. However, Beijing has expressed its desire to see an increase of its own influence and a reduction of American power in East Asia. China is constructing a military which can defeat American forces close to its own shores while slowly building expeditionary forces which could deploy into the Indian Ocean and beyond the first island chain in the Western Pacific. China's military developments strike at the heart of regional security in East Asia and have the potential to affect the entire international system.

THE PANDA CAN SWIM

The modernization and expansion of the People's Liberation Army (PLA) poses a direct challenge to security in East Asia. Unlike the previous threats posed by Nazi Germany, Imperial Japan and the Soviet Union, China has the potential to have a larger economy than the United States. As a study from the RAND Corporation asserts, "Over the next twenty years, China's gross domestic product (GDP) and defense budget could exceed those of the United States. If it chose, China could therefore become a more capable opponent than either the Soviet Union or Nazi Germany at their peak."[27] As was discussed in Chapter Three, Moscow's self-imposed isolation cut the Soviet Union off from the latest technological trends. For most of the Cold War, the Soviet Union was only about half as wealthy as the United States.[28] The leadership in Beijing does not have this problem. China has embraced globalization and uses the most advanced technology available to enhance its military power.[29] As China's power grows so will the need for the United States to remain committed to the defense of East Asia. This is not just charity work for people who wish to remain free from Beijing's influences, but rather American power helps stabilize one of the most important economic centers of the globe. By hedging against a belligerent China, the United States sends a message to Beijing that any aggressive acts in the region will not be worth the costs.

China's military modernization efforts continue to focus on developing capabilities to dissuade American intervention in the event China attacked Taiwan (officially known as the Republic of China).[30] However, China is also laying the foundation to project force beyond Taiwan Strait scenarios. The PLA is developing expeditionary capabilities with the eventual goal of projecting force into the Indian

Ocean and Persian Gulf. Much like the United States, China relies on energy bought overseas to maintain a strong economy. Unlike the United States, in China there is no mechanism for the average Chinese citizen to peacefully remove politicians from power. The CCP is perpetually worried that if economic conditions were ever to deteriorate too far China would succumb to violent uprisings.[31] Ensuring a steady supply of energy imports is not just necessary for economic growth but also essential for the CCP to maintain power.

In the mid-1980s, newly acquired wealth gave China the opportunity to improve its military and create a modern fighting force.[32] Between 1989 and 1994, China's military budget doubled. The 2005 budget was ten times greater than the 1989 budget.[33] Based on data released by the CCP, China's military budget grew on average 12.1 percent between 2000 – 2010.[34] The U.S. Department of Defense estimates that China's actual military spending for 2010 was over $160 billion.[35] China has been smart with its military budget, spending on programs specifically designed to prevent the United States from intervening in the Western Pacific. The PLA has invested heavily in technologies designed to cripple Taiwan, attack U.S. bases in Japan and prevent the United States Navy from conducting operations in the Western Pacific.[36]

Despite these military advancements, China has a strategic weakness in that it cannot protect its energy supplies which need to be imported from overseas. China's economy and therefore military power is increasingly reliant upon energy from the Persian Gulf. In 2009, China's net import of oil was 4.3 million barrels per day, surpassing Japan for the first time as the world's second largest importer of oil. [37] Approximately half of China's oil currently comes from the Persian Gulf. [38] Reliance upon Persian Gulf oil will only grow with time. By the end of this decade, this region will likely supply approximately 70 percent of China's oil needs.[39] By 2030, China will have to import 10 million barrels per day to meet its energy demand.[40] China is acutely aware of this problem and beginning to develop the military forces necessary to remedy the situation.

China is developing a Navy capable of successfully conducting operations around the Strait of Malacca, a vital transit port for world trade. The PLA(N) already has the capability to conduct anti-piracy missions off the coast of Africa. Although these operations are limited in scope, they will still provide China's Navy with valuable real-world lessons. By 2015, China's first aircraft carrier could be operational – a significant development even though mastering such a technology so that it can fight successfully in combat is still years away. To support a Navy capable of projecting power into the Indian Ocean, China is building a logistical supply chain from the South China Sea to the Persian Gulf. These bases and support facilities in Pakistan, Bangladesh and Myanmar will assist in sustaining operations designed to protect China's energy supply lanes. China is also trying to build a canal through Thailand, so its ships can avoid the narrow choke point of the Strait of Malacca. Analysts have described these bases as China's "String of Pearls." Currently, the United States protects the world's sea lanes and even China is powerless to challenge it. However, should the United States be unable to continue this role, or the PLA(N) develops to such an extent that it could challenge the United States Navy's supremacy of the seas, other nations would have to embark upon their own military buildup to ensure energy security.

The survival of the communist regime in Beijing is directly tied to the government's ability to bring economic prosperity to the nation. Since the 1996 Taiwan Strait crisis, the most likely scenario for war between China and the

United States dealt with Taiwan declaring independence or Taiwan taking some other act deemed unacceptable to Beijing. Going forward there is a greater danger that China or the United States will feel its economic security threatened. Issues over Taiwan deal with historic grievances, national honor and prestige – all symbolic factors which motivate nations into battle. However, economic issues deal with the living standards of citizens and the survival of governments – perfectly justifiable reasons for war.

MONEY AND POWER

The ongoing economic crisis is shifting the global economy away from free markets and towards a more hostile environment where governments intervene to save their industries at the expense of foreign companies. While this may be welcome news to workers in certain industries, ultimately this type of economic system is inefficient and causes economic conflict between nations. There is a danger that nations in the 21st century will view the world as a zero-sum competition where one nation's gain is another's loss. China and the United States are taking the first steps down this dangerous path.

The American led international system values open economies and disfavors protectionist measures. Multilateral intuitions help manage the global economy so that multi-national companies get treated equally before a given set of rules and regulations. The WTO helps mitigate economic disputes between countries, while the IMF and World Bank assist nations in financial trouble. These ideas and concepts were embraced and adhered to in the 1990s and 2000s for two reasons. First the United States and Western powers were the dominant economies and if nations wanted to be part of the global economy they had to play by American written rules. Second, these values and policies allowed the United States to achieve far more prosperity than any nation on Earth. Naturally, nations are going to want to emulate them. However, these factors are now changing. It is widely perceived that only through government intervention and investment can economies be competitive in the 21st century. From the sovereign wealth funds of the Arab monarchies, state owned energy companies in Russia and China and the United States' investment in "green technology," government intervention has made a comeback.

Discussion over government intervention in the markets is usually concerned with domestic politics and the ideological direction of the country. Should there be less or more government in the economic life of the United States has been a subject of debate for decades. Due to the economic transition underway, it is also important to ask the question - what effects will U.S. government activism in the markets have overseas? This question must be answered in order to avoid potential retaliatory acts by foreign governments whose own domestic industries may be affected by actions taken in Washington D.C.

The ultimate problem with government intervention in the economy is that the goals of intervention are more political than economic. Markets are ruthlessly efficient so much so that oftentimes governments feel the need to step in and prevent what they see as an unacceptable socio-economic market outcome. The state has different tools to protect its domestic industries from the downsides of foreign trade. As Ian Bremmer, President of the risk management firm the Eurasia Group has noted, nations can "require licenses that apply mainly to imported goods, limited imports to a small number of ports of entry, impose difficult- (or impossible-) to-meet public-health or safety standards on particular imported products, or block them on environmental grounds. It can direct local banks to favor domestic over foreign borrowers."[41] Some of these actions have already been used to minimize the negative effects of the global recession and financial crisis. French President Nicolas Sarkozy and German Chancellor Angela Merkel asked companies which received government aid to close down factories outside of their respective countries first.[42] Not only did the United States intervene to save its domestic automobile industry, but so did nations in Europe as well as Canada, South Korea, Russia and Brazil.[43] The problem with these policies is that when market outcomes "are significantly shaped by the policies of nations…it creates a severe system problem. The market then tilts toward a system of competitive, predatory competition between governments seeking to protect and subsidize profits and jobs at home."[44] Not only will the economies suffer in the long run, but governments will increasingly become more hostile towards each other in order to gain a competitive edge for their domestic industries. Failure to achieve the desired economic results can eventually lead nations to blame foreign countries for their domestic problems.

It is not difficult to develop a political narrative designed to paint China as the reason for the United States' economic woes. China continually purchases dollars as a means of keeping its own currency depreciated. These investments resulted in China holding over three trillion dollars in foreign exchange reserves, a trillion of which is treasury securities (U.S. debt).[45] China invested these holdings back into the United States. This had the effect of keeping interest rates low which contributed to the housing bubble and subsequent economic crisis. In addition, the manipulation of the Yuan allows China to make goods cheaper than American factories, contributing to the outsourcing of jobs overseas. Senator Chuck Schumer (D-NY), in discussing the Chinese Yuan, opined, "China's currency manipulation is like a boot to the throat of our recovery,"[46] China's economic power has not gone unnoticed by the American public. Fifty- two percent of Americans already perceive China to be the leading economic power in the world.[47] When Americans were asked, "What one country anywhere in the world do you consider to be the United States' greatest enemy today?" China tied with North Korea for second.[48] This is a disturbing trend, considering China's policies are far more benign than the Stalinist regime in North Korea. In addition, China's currency has risen over 31 percent in the past seven years against the U.S. dollar reducing much of the price advantage Chinese products had against American manufactured goods.[49] However, these are just symptoms of a much deeper distrust between the two nations.

Continued economic stagnation could cause the United States to act on this narrative to the detriment of all parties involved. China's trade imbalances with the United States have the potential to undermine globalization and cause the United States to place trade barriers on Chinese goods.[50] In 2010, the United States House of Representatives voted overwhelmingly, in a bipartisan effort, to give the President authority to impose tariffs on virtually all Chinese goods. [51] Although the Senate did not take up the measure, it is a bad sign of where the U.S.-Sino relationship is heading. If such measures were ever enacted, China would certainly retaliate possibly by dumping U.S. dollar holdings, wrecking the United States economy. Although this is only conjecture, that is the point, there is no telling where a trade war would lead. Such an event has the potential to pull other countries into the economic conflict as China and the United States would offer incentives for nations to pick one partner over the other. It is not unthinkable that alliances would form around economic interests creating the types of rivalries which precede a great power war.

The complicated nature of the U.S.-Sino relationship makes it difficult to predict exactly what would precede a conflict. It is fashionable to relate this relationship to the Anglo-Germany rivalry during the early 20th century.[52] German unification in the late 1800s changed the security dynamics of the continent. Germany's increase in power became a threat to British interests. This threat was most evident in Germany's desire to build a navy capable of rivaling the British Royal Navy.[53] Eventually, an inflexible system of alliances developed on the continent which helped contribute to the outbreak of the First World War. History does not repeat itself but human nature does.[54] There is a school of thought which says that the systematic nature of international politics makes conflict between a rising power and a status quo power likely.[55] This is the "tragedy of great power politics."[56] China's military buildup is a threat to American influence. The motives or desires of the present or future governments in Beijing are not relative to this line of reasoning. Not even the system of government, if it is democratic or authoritarian, matters. Inevitably, two large powers will cause an increase in security competition eventually leading to great power war reminiscent of the early 20th century.

Perhaps this line of reasoning is correct or maybe it will prove completely wrong. As Yogi Berra supposedly said, "It's tough to make predictions, especially about the future." Since no one can be certain of what will happen in East Asia, it is prudent for the United States to keep the security commitments which have been a cornerstone of peace in the region for over sixty years.

CONCLUSION

A return of great power war may appear unlikely and arguments to guard against it alarmist, but life is full of surprises. In international politics, those surprises are typically unpleasant. About one hundred years ago technological innovations such as steam power, railroads and the telegraph integrated the world like never before. In 1910, author Norman Angell wrote a best seller, *The Great Illusion*, which made the convincing case that the internationalization of credit made another war less likely.[57] These opinions were widely accepted in both Germany and Great Britain. Of course, history did not progress as comfortably and safely as people expected.

Peace, like anything precious, must be constantly guarded and cared for. Sixty years ago the United States defeated aspiring hegemons Germany and Japan. In their defeat a new international system was created that contained the Soviet Union and created economic prosperity. Twenty years ago the United States oversaw the dismantling of the Warsaw Pact, the breakup of the Soviet Union and a reunited Europe whole and free.

While the exact circumstances of future diplomatic crises are unknown, it is helpful to remember the different philosophical foundations of the international systems which helped bring on the Second World War and which helped avoid a third global war. During the 1930s nations shut themselves off from one another and tried to achieve success at the expense of their neighbors' economic and political security. The result was a series of crises which eventually led to global war. After the Second World War, the United States founded a new international system which allowed nations to prosper without resorting to force. This system only survived due to American military power containing the Soviet Union. Eventually, the Soviet Union lost the Cold War because communism proved a terrible means of organizing society and it could no longer continue an arms race with the vastly richer United States. In wake of the Soviet Union's demise, the United States kept its military forward deployed as a means of reassuring allies and to prevent other nations from altering the security dynamics of their region. Even with the current challenges facing the United States, there is no reason these policies cannot continue. The United States need only fix its current debt problems, resist the temptation to have the government intervene in domestic industries and have an unmatched military capable of handling any challenge. If the United States is going to continue to be the guardian of the international system, it must have the military power to defeat any nation which threatens to alter the security dynamics of Europe, the Middle East and East Asia. If the United States fails in this respect, the entire system will come undone likely leading to a great power war.

When President Wilson gave his famous "Peace Without Victory" speech he asked the American people, "Is the present war a struggle for a just and secure peace, or only for a new balance of power? If it be only for a new balance of power, who will guarantee, who can guarantee, the stable equilibrium of the new arrangement?"[58] Nearly a century after the Great War and six decades after the Second World

War, it can be said confidently that Untied States of America maintains a balance of power, a balance of power which favors peace. American power has been a presence for so long it is often taken for granted as if it were a natural feature of international relations. It is not natural – it is the policies of a single nation trying to advance human society beyond the death and destruction which has plagued mankind for all of recorded history. American power remains the best hope for peace.

NOTES

MY PURPOSE

[1] Nye, Joseph S. "East Asian Security: The Case for Deep Engagement." Foreign Affairs. July 1, 1995. Accessed February 27, 2012. http://www.foreignaffairs.com/articles/51210/joseph-s-nye-jr/east-asian-security-the-case-for-deep-engagement.

[2] Robert Gilpin argued how the relationship between nations is best understood as a series of different systems influenced by the most powerful countries. Robert Gilpin, *War and Change in World Politics*, (New York, New York: Cambridge University Press, 1981)

CHAPTER ONE

[1] For a comparison of President Woodrow Wilson's liberal view of the world and Europe's traditional balance of power viewpoints see Henry Kissinger, *Diplomacy*, (New York: Simon and Schuster, 1994) 218 – 245

[2] "It was no easy matter to be generous toward France…Nevertheless the statesmen at Vienna concluded that Europe would be safer if France were relatively satisfied rather than resentful and disaffected." Ibid, 81-83

[3] Italics added by author. Woodrow Wilson: "Address to a Joint Session of Congress Requesting a Declaration of War Against Germany," April 2, 1917. Online by Gerhard Peters and John T. Woolley, The American Presidency Project

[4] The Woodrow Wilson Presidential Library, "Woodrow Wilson: Address to the Senate on Peace Without Victory 22 Jan. 1917" http://www.woodrowwilson.org/

[5] Kissinger, *Diplomacy*, 52

[6] Woodrow Wilson Presidential Library, "Woodrow Wilson: Address at the University of Paris, France, 21 December, 1918" http://www.woodrowwilson.org/

[7] Donald Kagan, *On the Origins of War and the Preservation of Peace*, (New York: Random House, Inc, 1995) 288-289

[8] Quoted in, Edward Hallett Carr, *The Twenty Years' Crisis, 1919 – 1939, An Introduction to the Study of International Relations,* (New York: Harper & Row Publishers, 1939) 35

[9] John Keegan, *The First World War,* (New York: Alfred A. Knopf, 1999) 5, For the populations of the Great Powers from 1890 – 1938 see Paul Kennedy, *The Rise and Fall of the Great Powers,* (New York: Random House, 1987) 199

[10] Keegan, 7

[11] Winston S. Churchill, *The Second World War, The Gathering Storm,* (New York: Houghton Mifflin Company, 1948) 4

[12] Ibid, 5

[13] Ibid, 5

[14] André Tardieu, *The Truth About the Treaty,* (London: Hodder and Stoughton, 1921) 164

[15] Knock, 221 – 222

[16] "Wilson rejected the idea that international conflicts had structural causes." Kissinger, *Diplomacy,* 232-233

[17] Woodrow Wilson: "Address to a Joint Session of Congress Requesting a Declaration of War Against Germany," April 2, 1917. Online by Gerhard Peters and John T. Woolley, The American Presidency Project. http://www.presidency.ucsb.edu/ws/?pid=65366.

[18] For a discussion on how Wilson's post-war goals were based on the assumption that Europe was on the verge of a "democratic revolution" see G. John Ikenberry, *After Victory: Institutions, Strategic Restraint, and the Rebuilding of Order After Major Wars,* (New Jersey: Princeton University Press, 2001) 155-160

[19] Carr, 31-36

[20] Ibid, 35

[21] "It was widely believed that Germany had voluntarily laid down her arms when Wilson offered a reasonable settlement of all strife." Hajo Holborn, *A History of Modern Germany 1840-1945*, (New York: 1969) 561

[22] Ibid, 561

[23] Kissinger, *Diplomacy*, 241

[24] Donald Kagan, *On the Origins of War and the Preservation of Peace*, (New York: Random House, Inc, 1995) 289-290

[25] Ibid, 290

[26] Yale Law School, Lillian Goldman Law Library, The Avalon Project, The Versailles Treaty, June 28, 1919 : Part VIII, *Accessed 8 May 2012:* http://avalon.law.yale.edu/imt/partviii.asp

[27] "Russia fell out of Europe and cease to exist , for the time being, as a great power." A.J.P Taylor, *The Origins of the Second World War,* (New York: Simon and Schuster, Inc, 1961) 20-21

[28] Ibid, 21

[29] Kissinger, *Diplomacy*, 241

[30] Dani Rodrik, *The Globalization Paradox: Democracy and the Future of the World Economy,* (New York: W.W. Norton & Company, Inc.) 24-46

[31] Kennedy, 281

[32] Ibid, 279

[33] Ibid, 279

[34] See the concluding chapter of Charles P. Kindleberger, *The World In Depression 1929 – 1939,* (California: University of California Press, 1986) 288-305

[35] For a summary of the tariff problems of the 1920s and the failed efforts to reduce them see Ibid, 61 – 65

[36] By the time of the 1933 World Economic Conference, "the cosmopolitan world order had dissolved into various rivaling subunits: a sterling block, based upon

British trade patterns and enhanced by the 'imperial preferences' of the 1932 Ottawa Conference: a gold block, led by France; a yen block, dependent upon Japan, in the Far East; a U.S.-led dollar block (after Roosevelt also went off gold); and, completely detached from these convulsions, a USSR steadily building 'socialism in one country'", Kennedy, *Rise and Fall...*, 283

[37] Rodrik, 45

[38] Of course there are a range of arguments on exactly why Japan went to war. My argument is that the global order made these nations more inclined to be unsatisfied with their place within the hierarchy of nations and therefore the use of force was a more attractive option compared to nations who were satisfied. For different arguments on this subject see, Michael A. Barnhart, "*Japan Prepares for Total War: The Search for Economic Security, 1919-1941,* (New York: Cornell University Press, 1987) and John Toland, *The Rising Sun: The Decline and Fall of the Japanese Empire,* (New York: Random House, 1970 and 2003)

[39] David Calleo, *The German Problem Reconsidered: Germany and the World Order, 1870 to the Present,* (New York: 1978) 100 – 107

[40] Taylor, 91

[41] Kissinger, *Diplomacy,* 298 – 299

[42] Taylor, 92

[43] Kissinger, 300

[44] Ibid, 300

[45] Taylor, 95

[46] Kissinger, 304

[47] Churchill, 175

[48] Ibid, 257

[49] Ibid, 257

[50] Ibid, 257

[51] Ibid, 279 -283

[52] William Manchester, *The Last Lion: Winston Spencer Churchill, Visions of Glory 1874-1932*, (New York: Little, Brown and Company, 1983) 335

CHAPTER TWO

[1] Robert A. Pollard, *Economic Security and the Origins of the Cold War, 1945 – 1950* (New York: Columbia Press, 1985) 11 – 17

[2] Quotes from John Lewis Gaddis, *Spheres of Influence: The United States and Europe, 1945 – 1949*, reprinted in Charles S. Maier, Ed. *The Cold War in Europe, Era of a Divided Continent*, (Princeton, NJ: Markus Wiener Publishers, 1991 and 1996) 111

[3] "Most historians agree that postwar Soviet policies in Eastern Europe were the product of reconstruction needs, traditional foreign policy objectives, Stalinist ideology, and internal political imperatives." See Pollard 35 – 40.

[4] Ikenberry, *After Victory*, 163

[5] John Lewis Gaddis, *We Now Know: Rethinking Cold War History*, (New York, Oxford University Press, 1997) 30-33

[6] Quote from Gaddis, *We Now Know...*, 29-30

[7] Quote from Leffler, 143

[8] For a description and analysis of American power in 1945, see Kennedy, *The Rise and Fall...*357-359

[9] Robert Gilpin, *The Political Economy of International Relations*, (Princeton: Princeton University Press, 1987) 131 – 134

[10] For an explanation of why and how Bretton Woods ended, see Ibid..., 138 - 142

[11] Franklin D. Roosevelt and Winston S. Churchill, "The Atlantic Charter", August 14, 1941, The Avalon Project, Yale Law School, Accessed, May 6, 2012: http://avalon.law.yale.edu/wwii/atlantic.asp

[12] Ibid

[13] Quote from Pollard, 14

[14] Michael H. Hunt, *The American Ascendancy: How the United States Gained & Wielded Global Dominance*, (Chapel Hill: University of North Carolina Press) 165

[15] For an explanation of how the Bretton Woods System developed and worked until 1976, see Gilpin, *The Political Economy..*, 131-134

[16] Although the United States would play the dominant role in the IMF and the International Bank for Reconstruction and Development, "Morgenthau and White designed major roles in the system for Great Britain and the Soviet Union...the Americans and the British wished to avoid the disastrous mistake made at Versailles of excluding a major power." Pollard, 13

[17] Ibid, 15

[18] Quote from Ibid, 15

[19] For Stalin breaking the promises of Yalta see Conrad Black, *Franklin Delano Roosevelt: A Champion of Freedom,* (New York: Public Affairs, 2003) 1077 – 1083

[20] Gaddis, *We Now Know..,* 30 – 31

[21] Ibid, 13 – 15

[22] Ibid, 15

[23] Niall Ferguson, *Colossus,* (New York: Penguin Group, 2004) 77

[24] Ibid, 77

[25] Pollard, 84 – 87

[26] Ibid, 175

[27] Ibid, 90

[28] Ibid, 90

[29] Ibid, 104, also see Hunt, 166

[30] Leffler, 101

[31] Pollard, 175

[32] Leffler, 7

[33] Ibid, 7

[34] Leffler, 61

[35] John Lewis Gaddis, *The Cold War: A New History,* (New York: Penguin Group, 2005), 28 – 29

[36] Harry S. Truman: "Special Message to the Congress on Greece and Turkey: The Truman Doctrine," March 12, 1947. Online by Gerhard Peters and John T. Woolley, The American Presidency Project. http://www.presidency.ucsb.edu/ws/?pid=12846.

[37] Harry S. Truman, "Address on Foreign Economic Policy," Delivered at Baylor University, March 6 1947, The American Presidency Project, http://www.presidency.ucsb.edu/ws/index.php?pid=12842#axzz1V3vp08NF

[38] The George C. Marshall Foundation, *The Marshall Plan Speech, June 4, 1946,* Accessed 8 May 2012: http://www.marshallfoundation.org/library/index_av.html

[39] G. John Ikenberry, *Liberal Leviathan: The Origins, Crisis, and Transformation of the American World Order,* (New Jersey: Princeton University Press, 2011) 198

[40] Fergusson, 80-81

[41] Ikenberry, *Leviathan...,* 199

[42] Ikenberry, *After Victory...,* 194-199

[43] Ferguson, 80

[44] Pollard, 165

[45] Ibid, 165

[46] Nicolaus Mills, *Winning The Peace: The Marshall Plan & America's Coming of Age as a Superpower,* (New Jersey: John Wiley and Sons, Inc, 2008) 199

[47] Ibid, 200 – 201

[48] Ikenberry, *Leviathan,* Chapter 5: 159-219

CHAPTER THREE

[1] Stephen Kotkin, *Armageddon Averted: The Soviet Collapse 1970-2000.* (New York, New York: Oxford University Press, 2008) 15 – 19

[2] Stephen G. Brooks and William C. Wohlforth, "Power, Globalization, and the End of the Cold War", *International Security,* Vol. 25, No. 3 (Winter 2000/01) 34 – 37

[3] Ibid, 36 – 37

[4] Vladislav M. Zubok, *A Failed Empire, The Soviet Union In The Cold War From Stalin to Gorbachev,* (Chapel Hill: The University of North Carolina Press,2007, 2009) 279

[5] "Gorbachev did not want to depart from the centralized planned economy. Years later, he explained that he had first wanted to use the existing state and party mechanisms for industrial modernization and only after that was accomplished, in the early 1990s, 'prepare the conditions for a radical economic reform.'" Ibid, 279

[6] Ibid, 279-280

[7] Brooks and Wohlforth, "Power, Globalization…5-33

[8] William Easterly and Stanley Fischer, "The Soviet Economic Decline, Historical and Republican Data", The World Bank, April 1994

[9] Ibid 22-23

[10] Ibid, 23

[11] Ibid, 18

[12] "It is clear now that these were the terminal excesses of a declining empire, but they did not seem so at the time." John Lewis Gaddis, *Strategies of Containment,* (New York, New York: Oxford University Press, 1982, 2005), 348

[13] Tom Clancy with General Fred Ranks, Jr. (RET.) *Into the Storm: A Study in Command,* (New York: G.P. Putnam's Sons, 1997) 85

[14] Jonathan M. House, *Combined Arms Warfare in the Twentieth Century* (Kansas: University Press of Kansas, 2001) 240

[15] "Minefields...antitank guided missiles at long range and faster firing tank guns at short range" were expected to compensate for the lack of personnel. Ibid, 240

[16] Interviewed by Daryl G. Kimball and Miles A. Pomper., "Interview with Nuclear Threat Initiative Co-Chairman Sam Nunn", *Arms Control Association*, January 24, 2008, Accessed 8 May 2012: http://www.armscontrol.org/print/2836

[17] Kiron K. Skinner, Annelise Anderson and Martin Anderson, *Reagan: In His Own Hand*, (New York: Simon and Schuster, 2001) 31

[18] Ronald Reagan, *An American Life*, (New York: Simon and Schuster, 1990) 267
[19] Gaddis, *Strategies of Containment*, 356 and 371-373

[20] William P. Clark, National Security Decision Directive-75, January 17, 1983 Accessed 10 May, 2012: Via Federation of American Scientists, http://www.fas.org/irp/offdocs/nsdd/nsdd-75.pdf

[21] I used 2005 dollars to put the amount spend in a more understandable context. Office of Management and Budget, Historical Tables, "Budget of the U.S. Government", Table 6.1, Composition of Outlays – 1940 – 2015

[22] For a history of the U.S. involvement in Afghanistan during the Soviet invasion, Steven Coll, *Ghost Wars: The Secret History of the CIA, Afghanistan and Bin Laden, From the Soviet Invasion to September 10, 2011,* (New York: Penguin Group, 2004) Chapters 2-9, pages 38-186.

[23] Philip Taubman, "Soviets List Afghan War Toll: 13, 310 Dead, 35,478 wounded," *New York Times, May 26, 1988,* Accessed 8 May 2012: http://www.nytimes.com/1988/05/26/world/soviet-lists-afghan-war-toll-13310-dead-35478-wounded.html

[24] Ronald Reagan: "Remarks at the Annual Convention of the National Association of Evangelicals in Orlando, Florida ," March 8, 1983. Online by Gerhard Peters and John T. Woolley, The American Presidency Project. http://www.presidency.ucsb.edu/ws/?pid=41023.

[25] Peggy Noonan, *When Character Was King,* (New York, New York: Viking, 2001), 288

[26] Robert Gates, *From the Shadows: The Ultimate Insiders Story of Five Presidents and How they Won the Cold War,* (New York: Simon and Schuster, 1996) 266

[27] For more on Gorbachev's thoughts on SDI see Zubok, 287

[28] Anatoly S. Chernyaev, *My Six Years With Gorbachev* (University Park: Pennsylvania State University Press, 2000) 83-84

[29] Brooks and Wohlforth, "Power, Globalization..." 36

[30] Kotkin, *Armageddon Averted,* 63

[31] Brooks and Wohlforth, "Power, Globalization..." 37

[32] Mann, 241

[33] Ibid 243

[34] Ibid 243

[35] Ibid 243

[36] Ibid, 244. Also see Gaddis, *The Cold War,* 233-234

[37] Michael Mandelbaum, *The Ideas That Conquered The World: Peace, Democracy, And Free Markets In The Twenty-First Century,* (New York: Public Affairs, 2002, 2003), 48

[38] Ibid, 72

[39] Henry Kissinger, *The White House Years,* (Boston, Toronto: Little, Brown and Company, 1979), 183

[40] "When he came to power, Gorbachev still believed in the Soviet system as it had evolved...He was convinced that the instrument to achieve these changes would be the Communist Party itself." Jack F. Matlock, Jr, *Reagan and Gorbachev: How the Cold War Ended* (New York: Random House, 2004) 110

[41] Ibid, 316

[42] Ambassador Matlock gives Gorbachev ultimate credit for ending the Cold War, more so than George Bush or Ronald Reagan, Ibid, 318

[43] Kotkin, 62 – 67

[44] Ibid, 67 – 73

[45] Zubok, 318 – 321

[46] "We (United States) didn't know at the time, for instance, that at the Warsaw Pact meeting at the end of May 1987, Gorbachev had also said that the Soviets would not intervene militarily in Eastern Europe." Gates, 423

[47] Zubok, 319

[18] Mikhail Gorbachev, *On My Country and the World,* (New York: Columbia University Press, 2000) 206

CHAPTER FOUR

[1] "No system of sovereign states has ever contained one state with comparable material preponderance." Stephen G. Brooks and William C. Wohlforth, *World Out of Balance: International Relations and the Challenge of American Primacy,* (New Jersey: Princeton University Press, 2008) 1

[2] Paul Kennedy, "The Eagle Has Landed," *Financial Times,* February 2, 2002

[3] Kenneth M. Waltz, "The Emerging Structure of International Relations" *International Security,* Vol. 18, No. 2. (Autumn, 1993), 44-79

[4] Derek Chollett and James Goldgeier, *America Between the Wars: From 11/9 to 9/11, The Misunderstood Years Between The Fall of the Berlin Wall and the Start of the War on Terror,* (New York: Public Affairs, 2008) 44

[5] PBS, 'Excerpts From 1992 Draft "Defense Planning Guidance"', Frontline, Accessed 8 May 2012: http://www.pbs.org/wgbh/pages/frontline/shows/iraq/etc/wolf.html

[6] Quote from Chollett and Goldgeier, 45

[7] Ibid, 45

[8] Patrick E. Tyler, "Lone Superpower Plan: Ammunition for Critics, *The New York Times,* March 10, 1992 Accessed 8 May 2012:
http://www.nytimes.com/1992/03/10/world/lone-superpower-plan-ammunition-for-critics.html?pagewanted=all

[9] John J. Mearsheimer, "Back to the Future: Instability in Europe After the Cold War," *International Security,* Vol. 15, No. 1(Summer 1990), 5-56

[10] Mandelbaum, *The Ideas...,* 152-153

[11] Quote from Ibid, 153

[12] Barry Posen, "Command of the Commons," *International Security,* Vol 28, Issue 1, 5-46, Summer 2003

[13] Ibid 8-9

[14] John J. Mearsheimer, "The Future of the American Pacifier," *Foreign Affairs,* September/October 2001, 46-61

[15] Charles A Kupchan, *The End of the American Era,* (New York: Random House 2002) 119 – 160

[16] Department of Defense, ACTIVE DUTY MILITARY PERSONNEL STRENGTHS BY REGIONAL AREA AND BY COUNTRY (309A) SEPTEMBER 30, 2011

[17] Chollett and Goldgeier, 124 – 135

[18] Mandelbaum, *Ideas...,* 130

[19] Philip Zelikow and Condoleeza Rice, *Germany Unified and Europe Transformed, A Study in Statecraft,* (Cambridge Massachusetts and London, England: Harvard University Press, 1995, 1997) 96-98

[20] Margaret Thatcher, *Statecraft, Strategies For A Changing World,* (New York: Harper Collins, 2002) 2

[21] Donald Rumsfeld, *Known and Unknown, A Memoir,* (New York: Penguin Group, 2011) 301 – 304

[22] North Atlantic Treaty Organization, "Financial and Economic Data Related to NATO Defence", Table 3, Defense Expenditures as a percentage of Gross Domestic Product, 10 March 2011

[23] "If the United States removed its security umbrella from over western Europe, Germany would likely move to acquire its own nuclear arsenal." John J. Mearsheimer, "The Future of the American Pacifier", *Foreign Affairs*, September/October 2001, 46 – 61

[24] Mandelbaum, *Ideas...*, 148 -155

[25] Aaron L. Friedberg, *A Contest for Supremacy, China, America, and the Struggle for Mastery in Asia,* (New York and London: W.W. Norton and Company, 2011) Chapter Three: From Containment to Alignment, 58-87

[26] Chollett and Goldgeier, 137

[27] Ibid, 137

[28] Associated Press, "China Wins Historic Trade Deal, Senate Grants Permanent Normal Status", 19 September 2000

[29] Michael Wines, "China's Economic Power Unsettles Neighbors", *The New York Times* December 9, 2009, Accessed 8 May 2012: http://www.nytimes.com/2009/12/10/world/asia/10jakarta.html?_r=2&hp=&pagewanted=1

[30] Jimmy Carter: "The State of the Union Address Delivered Before a Joint Session of the Congress. ," January 23, 1980. Online by Gerhard Peters and John T. Woolley, The American Presidency Project. http://www.presidency.ucsb.edu/ws/?pid=33079.

[31] Ibid

[32] Richard N. Hass, *War of Necessity, War of Choice, A Memoir of Two Iraq Wars,* (New York, London, Toronto, Sydney: Simon and Schuster, 2009) 132

[33] Sandra Mackey, *The Reckoning: Iraq and the Legacy of Saddam Hussein,* (New York: W.W. Norton and Company, Inc.) 278

[34] Hass, 132

[35] Ibid, 132

[36] Chollett and Goldgier, 181

[37] Ibid, 185

[38] Ibid, 189-194

[39] H.R.4655 -- Iraq Liberation Act of 1998, 105th Congress (1997-1998)

[40] Department of Defense, "Press Conference, DESERT FOX Briefing with Secretary Cohen and Gen. Zinni", 21 Dec 98, Accessed 8 May 2012: http://www.defense.gov/transcripts/transcript.aspx?transcriptid=1792, also see Dr. Mark J. Conversino, "Operation Desert Fox: Effectiveness with Unintended Effects," Air and Space Power Journal-Chronicles Online Journal, 13 July 2005, Accessed 8 May 2012: http://www.airpower.au.af.mil/airchronicles/cc/conversino.html

[41] William J. Clinton: "Address to the Nation Announcing Military Strikes on Iraq," December 16, 1998. Online by Gerhard Peters and John T. Woolley, The American Presidency Project. http://www.presidency.ucsb.edu/ws/?pid=55414.

[42] Ibid

[43] George W. Bush, *Decision Points,* (New York: Crown Publishers, 2010) 229

[44] Donald Rumsfeld, *Known and Unknown,* (New York: Penguin Group, 2011) 422

[45] Ibid, 422

[46] Ibid, 422-423

[47] Sharon A. Squassoni, *Iraq: U.N. Inspections for Weapons of Mass Destruction,* Congressional Research Service, Updated: October 7, 2003

[48] George Washington University, "U.S. Intelligence and the Indian Bomb", The National Security Archive, Document 39: Director of Central Intelligence, Jeremiah News Conference, June 2, 1998, Accessed 8 May 2012: http://www.gwu.edu/~nsarchiv/NSAEBB/NSAEBB187/IN39.pdf

[49] "Questions remain about the status of Iraq's weaponization program at the time of the allied bombing campaign in January 1991, when most activities were halted. Nevertheless, the Action Team inspectors have concluded that with the accelerated effort under the crash program, Iraq could have finished a nuclear explosive design by the end of 1991, if certain technical problems were overcome." David Albright and Khidhir Hamza, "Iraq's Reconstitution of Its Nuclear Weapons Program", *Arms Control Today*, October 1998

[50] "For him, it was critical that he was seen as still the strong, defiant Saddam. He thought that (faking having the weapons) would prevent the Iranians from reinvading Iraq," said Piro. CNN.com, "Agent: Hussein was surprised U.S. invaded", January 27, 2008, Accessed 8 May 2012: http://articles.cnn.com/2008-01-27/us/saddam.cbs_1_saddam-hussein-wmd-fbi-agent?_s=PM:US

[51] "He wanted to pursue all of WMD ... to reconstitute his entire WMD program." Ibid

[52] Thom Shanker and Steven Lee Myers, "U.S. Planning Troop Buildup in Gulf After Exit from Iraq", *The New York Times*, October 29, 2011

[53] Paul Kennedy, "Back to Normalcy," *The New Republic*, December 21, 2010

CHAPTER FIVE

[1] Gideon Rachman, *Zero-Sum Future: American Power in an Age of Anxiety,* (New York: Simon and Schuster, 2011) 7

[2] Kennedy, "Back to Normalcy"

[3] Christopher Layne, "Graceful Decline: The end of the Pax Americana," *The American Conservative*, May 01, 2010

[4] G20 London Summit, Leaders' Statement, Parliamentary Conference on the Global Economic Crisis, 2 April 2009

[5] "A win-win world is giving way to a zero-sum world." Rachman, *Zero-Sum Future,* 4

[6] Martin E. Dempsey, General, United States Army, Chairman, Joint Chiefs of Staff, "Joint Operational Access Concept," 17 January 2012

[7] $470 billion is the amount of money actually spent. Approximately $700 billion was originally authorized. Department of the Treasury, Daily TARP Update, May 4, 2012, Accessed 5 May 2012: http://www.treasury.gov/initiatives/financial-stability/briefing-room/reports/tarp-daily-summary-report/Pages/default.aspx

[8] Congressional Budget Office, *The Budget and Economic Outlook: Fiscal Years 2011 to 2021*, January 2011, 1, Also see Fiscal Year 2012, Historical Tables, Budget of the U.S. Government

[9] National Bureau of Economic Research, US Business Cycle Expansions and Contractions, Accessed 8 May 2012: http://www.nber.org/cycles.html

[10] Bureau of Economic Analysis, Table 1.1.1. Percent Change From Preceding Period in Real Gross Domestic Product, Revised December 22, 2011

[11] The Washington Post has a user friendly budget graphic that allows the viewer to see the history of government spending Washington Post, "Taking Apart the Federal Budget", Accessed 8 May 2012: http://www.washingtonpost.com/wp-srv/special/politics/budget-2010/

[12] THE NATIONAL COMMISSION ON FISCAL RESPONSIBILITY AND REFORM, *The Moment of Truth*, December 2010, http://www.fiscalcommission.gov/sites/fiscalcommission.gov/files/documents/The MomentofTruth12_1_2010.pdf

[13] Congressional Budget Office, *Long-Term Budget Outlook*, 2011

[14] Ibid

[15] Ibid

[16] Amy Belasco, *The Cost of Iraq, Afghanistan and Other Global War on Terror Operations Since 9/11,* Congressional Research Service, March 29, 2011

[17] Ibid, 1

[18] Numbers compiled using the Office of Management and Budget, Historic Tables

[19] National Intelligence *Council, Global Trends, 2025: A Transformed World,* November 2008, http://www.dni.gov/nic/PDF_2025/2025_Global_Trends_Final_Report.pdf

[20] Robert Gilpin, *War and Change in World Politics*, (New York, New York: Cambridge University Press, 1981)

[21] Goldman Sachs, *Dreaming with BRICS: The Path to 2050. Global Economics*, (99): 1 October 2003, Accessed 8 May 2012: http://www2.goldmansachs.com/ideas/brics/book/99-dreaming.pdf

[22] PricewaterhouseCoopers, *Convergence, Catch-Up and Overtaking: How the balance of world economic power is shifting*, January 2010 Accessed 8 May 2012: http://www.ukmediacentre.pwc.com/imagelibrary/downloadMedia.ashx?MediaDetailsID=1626

[23] Ibid

[24] Kennedy, *Rise and Fall*, xxiii

[25] Republic of Turkey, Ministry of Foreign Affairs, *Joint Declaration of the Ministers of Foreign Affairs of Turkey, Iran and Brazil*, May 17, 2010, Accessed 8 May 2012: http://www.mfa.gov.tr/17_05_2010-joint-declaration-of-the-ministers-of-foreign-affairs-of-turkey_-iran-and-brazil_.en.mfa

[26] Reuters, "U.S.: Turkey-Brazil nuclear swap deal with Iran is too little too late" 29 May 2010

[27] James Dobbins, David C. Gompert, David A. Shlapak and Andrew Scobell, *Conflict with China: Prospects, Consequences, and Strategies for Deterrence*, RAND Corporation, 2011, 1

[28] Mearsheimer, *Tragedy*...398. Also see table 3.5 Relative Share of Superpower Wealth, 1945-90, 74

[29] Friedberg, 232-237

[30] Annual Report to Congress, *Military and Security Developments Involving the People's Republic of China*, 2011, 2

[31] The fear China's rulers have of domestic uprisings is discussed at length in Susan L. Shirk, *China: Fragile Superpower*, (New York: Oxford University Press, 2008)

[32] Avery Goldstein, *Rising to the Challenge, China's Grand Strategy and International Security*, (Sanford California: Sanford University Press, 2005) 56 – 58

[33] Annual Report to Congress, 31

[34] Ibid, 41

[35] Ibid, 41

[36] Wendell Minnick, "Rand Study Suggest U.S. Loses War With China", *Defense News,* October 16, 2009 Accessed 6 May 2012: http://www.defensenews.com/story.php?i=3774348, Also see the actual study here: http://www.defenseindustrydaily.com/files/2008_RAND_Pacific_View_Air_Comb at_Briefing.pdf

[37] Energy Information Agency, "Country Analysis Briefs: China," November 2010, Accessed May 6, 2012: http://www.eia.gov/cabs/china/pdf.pdf

[38] Energy Information Agency, "China." Updated May 2011, Accessed May 6, 2012: http://www.eia.gov/cabs/china/Full.html

[39] Philip McCrum, "Special Report: China and The Gulf," The Gulf, May 30 – June 5, 2009, http://www.kuwaitchina.com/UserFiles/file/KCIC_in_the_Press/The%20Gulf_Chin a%20and%20the%20Gulf_Special%20Report_May%20Jun%2009.pdf

[40] Ibid

[41] For a discussion on "state capitalism" and its effect on international affairs see Ian Bremmer, *The End of the Free Market: Who Wins the War Between States and Corporations?* (New York: Penguin Group, 2010) 157

[42] Rachman, 194-195

[43] John Reed, "Back on the road", *Financial Times*, June 17, 2009. Accessed 20 May, 2012: http://www.ft.com/cms/s/0/0f821d34-5b64-11de-be3f-00144feabdc0.html#axzz1vSvX2wdy

[44] Stephen S. Cohen and J. Bradford DeLong, *The End Of Influence: What Happens When Other Countries Have the Money,* (New York: Basic Books, 2010) 11

[45] Wayne M. Morrison, "China's Holdings of Securities, Implications for the U.S. Economy", *Congressional Research Service,* September 26, 2011

[46] Reuters, "Washington Extra – Godilocks Geitner," September 16, 2010, http://blogs.reuters.com/frontrow/2010/09/16/washington-extra-goldilocks-geithner/

[47] Gallup, "China Surges in Americans' View of Top World Economy," February 14, 2011, Accessed 8 May 2012: http://www.gallup.com/poll/146099/China-Surges-Americans-Views-Top-World-Economy.aspx

[48] Iran came in first. Gallup, "Americans Continue to Rate Iran as Greatest U.S. Enemy," February 18, 2011, Accessed 8 May 2012: http://www.gallup.com/poll/146165/Americans-Continue-Rate-Iran-Greatest-Enemy.aspx

[49] Stella Dawson, "Politics Clash with Reality over China Currency," *Reuters,* April 13 2012

[50] Rodrik, 274-275

[51] David E. Sanger and Sewell Chan, "Eye on China: House Votes for Greater Tariff Powers", *The New York Times,* September 29, 2010 , Accessed 8 May 2012: http://www.nytimes.com/2010/09/30/business/30currency.html

[52] Kissinger discusses this analogy at length in the epilogue of his latest and possibly last work: Henry Kissinger, *On China,* (New York: Penguin Press, 2011) 314-530. Also see Fareed Zakaria, "China: Appease…or Contain? Speak Softly, Carry a Veiled Threat," *New York Times,* February 18, 1996, Accessed 8 May 2012: http://www.nytimes.com/1996/02/18/magazine/china-appease-or-contain-speak-softly-carry-a-veiled-threat.html?pagewanted=all&src=pm, and Walter Russell Meade, "In the Footsteps of the Kaiser: China Boosts US Power in Asia, *The American Interest,* September 26, 2010, Accessed 8 May 2012: http://blogs.the-american interest.com/wrm/2010/09/26/in-the-footsteps-of-the-kaiser-china-boosts-us-power-in-asia/

[53] Germany's naval buildup was "a naval race of unprecedented size and cost, a diplomatic revolution that saw the emergence of two antagonistic power blocs and, almost every scholar would agree, played a vital part in bringing on the war." Kagan, 137

[54] This delightful quote was obtained from John Toland, *The Rising Sun: The Decline and Fall of the Japanese Empire, 1936-1945,* (New York: Random House, Inc., 1970 and 1998) xv

[33] "China and the United States are destined to be adversaries as China's power grows." Mearsheimer, *Tragedy...*, 4

[56] "The Tragedy of Great Powers" is University of Chicago's John Mearsheimer's book on the international relations theory known as "offensive realism."

[57] Keegan, 10-18. Also see Norman Angel, *The Great Illusion – A Study of the Relation of Military Power to National Advantage,* (London: William Heinemann, 1912, first published in November 1909)

[58] The Woodrow Wilson Presidential Library, "Woodrow Wilson: Address to the Senate on Peace Without Victory 22 Jan. 1917" http://www.woodrowwilson.org/

BIBLIOGRAPHY

David Albright and Khidhir Hamza, "Iraq's Reconstitution of Its Nuclear Weapons Program", *Arms Control Today*, October 1998

Norman Angel, *The Great Illusion – A Study of the Relation of Military Power to National Advantage*, (London: William Heinemann, 1912, first published in November 1909)

Annual Report to Congress, *Military and Security Developments Involving the People's Republic of China*, 2011

Associated Press, "China Wins Historic Trade Deal, Senate Grants Permanent Normal Status", 19 September 2000

Michael A. Barnhart, "*Japan Prepares for Total War: The Search for Economic Security, 1919-1941*, (New York: Cornell University Press, 1987)

Amy Belasco, *The Cost of Iraq, Afghanistan and Other Global War on Terror Operations Since 9/11*, Congressional Research Service, March 29, 2011

Ian Bremmer, *The End of the Free Market: Who Wins the War Between States and Corporations?* (New York: Penguin Group, 2010)

Bureau of Economic Analysis, Table 1.1.1. Percent Change From Preceding Period in Real Gross Domestic Product, Revised December 22, 2011

Congressional Budget Office, *The Budget and Economic Outlook: Fiscal Years 2011 to 2021*

CNN.com, "Agent: Hussein was surprised U.S. invaded", January 27, 2008 http://articles.cnn.com/2008-01-27/us/saddam.cbs_1_saddam-hussein-wmd-fbi-agent?_s=PM:US

Conrad Black, *Franklin Delano Roosevelt: A Champion of Freedom*, (New York: Public Affairs, 2003)

Stephen G. Brooks and William C. Wohlforth, "Power, Globalization, and the End of the Cold War", *International Security*, Vol. 25, No. 3 (Winter 2000/01)

Stephen G. Brooks and William C. Wohlforth, *World Out of Balance: International Relations and the Challenge of American Primacy,* (New Jersey: Princeton University Press, 2008)

George W. Bush, *Decision Points,* (New York: Crown Publishers, 2010)
Jimmy Carter: "The State of the Union Address Delivered Before a Joint Session of the Congress. ," January 23, 1980. Online by Gerhard Peters and John T. Woolley, The American Presidency Project. http://www.presidency.ucsb.edu/ws/?pid=33079.

Winston S. Churchill, *The Second World War, Volume 1, The Gathering Storm,* (New York: Houghton Mifflin Company, 1948)

Tom Clancy with General Fred Ranks, Jr. (RET.) *Into the Storm: A Study in Command,* (New York: G.P. Putnam's Sons, 1997)

William P. Clark, National Security Decision Directive-75, January 17, 1983

William J. Clinton: "Address to the Nation Announcing Military Strikes on Iraq," December 16, 1998. Online by Gerhard Peters and John T. Woolley, The American Presidency Project. http://www.presidency.ucsb.edu/ws/?pid=55414.

Stephen S. Cohen and J. Bradford DeLong, *The End Of Influence: What Happens When Other Countries Have the Money,* (New York: Basic Books, 2010)

Derek Chollet and James Goldgeier, *America Between the Wars: From 11/9 to 9/11, The Misunderstood Years Between The Fall of the Berlin Wall and the Start of the War on Terror,* (New York: Public Affairs, 2008)

Congressional Budget Office, *Long-Term Budget Outlook,* 2011

Dr. Mark J. Conversino, "Operation Desert Fox: Effectiveness with Unintended Effects," Air and Space Power Journal-Chronicles Online Journal, 13 July 2005

Stella Dawson, "Politics Clash with Reality over China Currency," *Reuters,* April 13 2012

Martin E. Dempsey, General, United States Army, Chairman, Joint Chiefs of Staff, "Joint Operational Access Concept," 17 January 2012

Department of Defense, ACTIVE DUTY MILITARY PERSONNEL STRENGTHS BY REGIONAL AREA AND BY COUNTRY (309A) SEPTEMBER 30, 2011

James Dobbins, David C. Gompert, David A. Shlapak and Andrew Scobell, *Conflict with China: Prospects, Consequences, and Strategies for Deterrence*, RAND, 2011

William Easterly and Stanley Fischer, "The Soviet Economic Decline, Historical and Republican Data", The World Bank, April 1994

Energy Information Agency, "Country Analysis Briefs: China," November 2010, http://www.eia.gov/cabs/china/pdf.pdf

Energy Information Agency, "China." Updated May 2011, http://www.eia.gov/cabs/china/Full.html

Robert English and Elizabeth Tucker, translated and edited, Anaatoly Chernyaev, *My Six Years with Gorbachev,* (Pennsylvania: The Pennsylvania State University Press, 2000)

Niall Ferguson, *Colossus,* (New York: Penguin Group, 2004)

Aaron L. Friedberg, *A Contest for Supremacy, China, America, and the Struggle for Mastery in Asia,* (New York and London: W.W. Norton and Company, 2011) Chapter Three: From Containment to Alignment, 58-87

G20 London Summit, "Leaders' Statement, Parliamentary Conference on the Global Economic Crisis", 2 April 2009

John Lewis Gaddis, *Strategies of Containment,* (New York, New York: Oxford University Press, 1982,2005)

John Lewis Gaddis, *The Cold War: A New History,* (New York: Penguin Group, 2005)

John Lewis Gaddis, *We Now Know: Rethinking Cold War History,* (New York, Oxford University Press, 1997)

Gallup, "China Surges in Americans' View of Top World Economy," February 14, 2011, Accessed 8 May 2012: http://www.gallup.com/poll/146099/China-Surges-Americans-Views-Top-World-Economy.aspx

Gallup, "Americans Continue to Rate Iran as Greatest U.S. Enemy," February 18, 2011, http://www.gallup.com/poll/146165/Americans-Continue-Rate-Iran-Greatest-Enemy.aspx

Robert Gilpin, *War and Change in World Politics*, (New York, New York: Cambridge University Press, 1981)

Robert Gilpin, *The Political Economy of International Relations*, (Princeton: Princeton University Press, 1987)

Robert M. Gates, *From the Shadows: The Ultimate Insider's Story of Five Presidents and How They Won the Cold War*, (New York: Simon and Schuster Paperbacks, 1996)

Goldman Sachs, *Dreaming with BRICS: The Path to 2050. Global Economics*, (99): 1 October 2003, Accessed 8 May 2012: http://www2.goldmansachs.com/ideas/brics/book/99-dreaming.pdf

Mikhail Gorbachev, *On My Country and the World*, (New York: Columbia University Press, 2000)

Richard N. Haass, *War of Necessity, War of Choice: A Memoir of Two Iraq Wars*, (New York, London, Toronto, Sydney: Simon and Schuster Paperbacks, 2009)

Jonathan M. House, *Combined Arms Warfare in the Twentieth Century* (Kansas: University Press of Kansas, 2001)

Hajo Holborn, *A History of Modern Germany 1840-1945*, (New York: 1969)

H.R.4655 -- Iraq Liberation Act of 1998, 105th Congress (1997-1998)

Michael H. Hunt, *The American Ascendancy: How the United States Gained & Wielded Global Dominance*, (Chapel Hill: University of North Carolina Press)

G. John Ikenberry, *After Victory: Institutions, Strategic Restraint, and the Rebuilding of Order After Major Wars*, (Princeton: Princeton University Press, 2001)

G. John Ikenberry, *Liberal Leviathan: The Origins, Crisis, and Transformation of the American World Order*, (New Jersey: Princeton University Press, 2011)

Donald Kagan, *On The Origins of War and the Preservation of Peace*, (New York: Anchor Books, 1995)

John Keegan, *The First World War*, (New York: Alfred A. Knopf, 1999)

Paul Kennedy, *The Rise and Fall of the Great Powers,* (New York: Random House, 1987)

Paul Kennedy, "The Eagle Has Landed," *Financial Times,* February 2, 2002

Paul Kennedy, "Back to Normalcy," *The New Republic*, December 21, 2010

Daryl G. Kimball and Miles A. Pomper., "Interview with Nuclear Threat Initiative Co-Chairman Sam Nunn", *Arms Control Association*, January 24, 2008

Charles P. Kindleberger, *The World in Depression 1929-1939,* (California: University of California Press, 1973, Revised and Enlarged Edition 1986)

Henry Kissinger, *Diplomacy,* (New York: Simon and Schuster, 1994)

Henry Kissinger, *The White House Years*, (Boston, Toronto: Little, Brown and Company, 1979)

Henry Kissinger, *On China,* (New York: Penguin Press, 2011)

Thomas J. Knock, *To End All Wars, Woodrow Wilson and the Quest for a New World Order,* (New Jersey: Princeton University Press, 1992)

Stephen Kotkin, *Armageddon Averted, The Soviet Collapse 1970-2000.* (New York, New York: Oxford University Press, 2008)

Melvyn P. Leffler, *A Preponderance of Power: National Security, the Truman Administration, and the Cold War,* (Stanford: Stanford University Press, 1992)

Charles A Kupchan, *The End of the American Era,* (New York: Random House 2002) 119 – 160

Christopher Layne, "Graceful Decline: The end of the Pax Americana," *The American Conservative*, May 01, 2010

Charles S. Maier, Ed. *The Cold War in Europe: Era of a Divided Continent,* (Princeton: Markus Wiener Publishers, Inc. 1991, Updated and Expanded 1996)

Sandra Mackey, *The Reckoning: Iraq and the Legacy of Saddam Hussein,* (New York: W.W. Norton and Company, Inc. 2002)

Office of Management and Budget, Historical Tables, "Budget of the U.S. Government", Table 6.1, Composition of Outlays – 1940 – 2015

William Manchester, *The Last Lion: Winston Spencer Churchill, Visions of Glory 1874-1932,* (New York: Little, Brown and Company, 1983)

James Mann, *Rise of the Vulcans: A History of Bush's War Cabinet,* (New York: Penguin Group, 2004)

The George C. Marshall Foundation, *The Marshall Plan Speech, June 4, 1946, Accessed 8 May 2012: http://www.marshallfoundation.org/library/index_av.html*

Jack F. Matlock, Jr, *Reagan and Gorbachev: How the Cold War Ended* (New York: Random House, 2004)

Walter Russell Meade, "In the Footsteps of the Kaiser: China Boosts US Power in Asia, *The American Interests,* September 26, 2010, Accessed 8 May 2012: http://blogs.the-american interest.com/wrm/2010/09/26/in-the-footsteps-of-the-kaiser-china-boosts-us-power-in-asia

John J. Mearsheimer, *The Tragedy of Great Power Politics,* (New York: W.W. Norton and Company, Inc., 2001)

John J. Mearsheimer, "Back to the Future: Instability in Europe After the Cold War," *International Security,* Vol. 15, No. 1(Summer 1990), 5-56

John J. Mearsheimer, "The Future of the American Pacifier," *Foreign Affairs,* September/October 2001, 46-61

Charles L. Mee, Jr. *The Marshall Plan: The Launching of the Pax Americana,* (New York: Simon and Schuster, 1984)

Nicolaus Mills, *Winning The Peace: The Marshall Plan & America's Coming of Age as a Superpower,* (New Jersey: John Wiley and Sons, Inc, 2008)

Philip McCrum, "Special Report: China and The Gulf," *The Gulf,* May 30 – June 5, 2009, http://www.kuwaitchina.com/UserFiles/file/KCIC_in_the_Press/The%20Gulf_China%20and%20the%20Gulf_Special%20Report_May%20Jun%2009.pdf

Wendell Minnick, "Rand Study Suggest U.S. Loses War With China", *Defense News,* October 16, 2009 Accessed 6 May 2012: http://www.defensenews.com/story.php?i=3774348

Wayne M. Morrison, "China's Holdings of Securities, Implications for the U.S. Economy", *Congressional Research Service,* September 26, 2011

National Bureau of Economic Research, US Business Cycle Expansions and Contractions, http://www.nber.org/cycles.html

THE NATIONAL COMMISSION ON FISCAL RESPONSIBILITY AND REFORM, *The Moment of Truth,* December 2010, 11

North Atlantic Treaty Organization, "Financial and Economic Data Related to NATO Defence", Table 3, Defense Expenditures as a percentage of Gross Domestic Product, 10 March 2011

Peggy Noonan, *When Character Was King,* (New York, New York: Viking, 2001)

Nye, Joseph S. "East Asian Security: The Case for Deep Engagement." Foreign Affairs. July 1, 1995. Accessed February 27, 2012.

PBS, 'Excerpts From 1992 Draft "Defense Planning Guidance"', Frontline, http://www.pbs.org/wgbh/pages/frontline/shows/iraq/etc/wolf.html

Robert A. Pollard, *Economic Security and the Origins of the Cold War, 1945 – 1950* (New York: Columbia Press, 1985)

Barry Posen, "Command of the Commons," *International Security,* Vol 28, Issue 1, 5-46, Summer 2003

Ronald Reagan, *An American Life,* (New York: Simon and Schuster, 1990) 267.

PricewaterhouseCoopers, *"Convergence, Catch-Up and Overtaking: How the balance of world economic power is shifting",* January 2010

Gideon Rachman, *Zero-Sum Future: American Power in an Age of Anxiety,* (New York: Simon and Schuster, 2011)

Ronald Reagan: "Remarks at the Annual Convention of the National Association of Evangelicals in Orlando, Florida ," March 8, 1983. Online by Gerhard Peters and John T. Woolley, The American Presidency Project.

John Reed, "Back on the road", *Financial Times*, June 17, 2009

Reuters, "U.S.: Turkey-Brazil nuclear swap deal with Iran is too little too late" 29 May 2010

Reuters, "Washington Extra – Godilocks Geitner," September 16, 2010, http://blogs.reuters.com/frontrow/2010/09/16/washington-extra-goldilocks-geithner/

Dani Rodrik, *The Globalization Paradox: Democracy and the Future of the World Economy,* (New York: W.W. Norton and Company, Inc, 2011)

Donald Rumsfeld, *Known and Unknown: A Memoir,* (New York: Penguin Group, 2011)

David E. Sanger and Sewell Chan, "Eye on China: House Votes for Greater Tariff Powers", *The New York Times,* September 29, 2010, http://www.nytimes.com/2010/09/30/business/30currency.html

Elaine Sciolino, *The Outlaw State: Saddam Hussein's Quest for Power and the Gulf Crisis,* (New York: John Wiley & Sons, Inc, 1991)

Thom Shanker and Steven Lee Myers, "U.S. Planning Troop Buildup in Gulf After Exit from Iraq", *The New York Times*, October 29, 2011

Kiron K. Skinner, Annelise Anderson and Martin Anderson, *Reagan: In His Own Hand*, (New York: Simon and Schuster, 2001

André Tardieu, *The Truth About the Treaty,* (London: Hodder and Stoughton, 1921)

Philip Taubman, "Soviets List Afghan War Toll: 13, 310 Dead, 35,478 wounded," *New York Times, May 26, 1988*

A.J.P Taylor, *The Origins of the Second World War,* (New York: Simon and Schuster, Inc, 1961) 20-21

Margaret Thatcher, *Statecraft: Strategies For A Changing World,* (New York: Harper Collins, 2002)

Harry S. Truman: "Special Message to the Congress on Greece and Turkey: The Truman Doctrine," March 12, 1947. Online by Gerhard Peters and John T. Woolley, The American Presidency Project. http://www.presidency.ucsb.edu/ws/?pid=12846.

The American Presidency Project, Harry S. Truman, Address on Foreign Economic Policy, Delivered at Baylor University, March 6 1947, http://www.presidency.ucsb.edu/ws/index.php?pid=12842#axzz1V3vp08NF

John Toland, *The Rising Sun: The Decline and Fall of the Japanese Empire, 1936-1945,* (New York: Random House, Inc., 1970 and 1998)

Republic of Turkey, Ministry of Foreign Affairs, *Joint Declaration of the Ministers of Foreign Affairs of Turkey, Iran and Brazil,* May 17, 2010

Patrick E. Tyler, "Lone Superpower Plan: Ammunition for Critics, *The New York Times,* March 10, 1992 Accessed 8 May 2012: http://www.nytimes.com/1992/03/10/world/lone-superpower-plan-ammunition-for-critics.html?pagewanted=all

Yale Law School, Lillian Goldman Law Library, The Avalon Project, The Versailles Treaty, June 28, 1919 : Part VIII, *Accessed 8 May 2012:* http://avalon.law.yale.edu/imt/partviii.asp

Kenneth M. Waltz, "The Emerging Structure of International Relations*" International Security,* Vol. 18, No. 2. (Autumn, 1993), 44-79

Washington Post, "Taking Apart the Federal Budget", http://www.washingtonpost.com/wp-srv/special/politics/budget-2010/

George Washington University, "U.S. Intelligence and the Indian Bomb", The National Security Archive, Document 39: Director of Central Intelligence, Jeremiah News Conference, June 2, 1998, Accessed 8 May 2012: http://www.gwu.edu/~nsarchiv/NSAEBB/NSAEBB187/IN39.pdf

Woodrow Wilson: "Address to a Joint Session of Congress Requesting a Declaration of War Against Germany," April 2, 1917. Online by Gerhard Peters and John T. Woolley, The American Presidency Project

The Woodrow Wilson Presidential Library, "Woodrow Wilson: Address to the Senate on Peace Without Victory 22 Jan. 1917" http://www.woodrowwilson.org/

Woodrow Wilson Presidential Library, "Woodrow Wilson: Address at the University of Paris, France, 21 December, 1918" http://www.woodrowwilson.org/

Michael Wines, "China's Economic Power Unsettles Neighbors", *The New York Times* December 9, 2009

Fareed Zakaria, "China: Appease…or Contain? Speak Softly, Carry a Veiled Threat, *New York Times,* February 18, 1996

Philip Zelikow and Condoleeza Rice, *Germany Unified and Europe Transformed, A Study in Statecraft,* (Cambridge Massachusetts and London, England: Harvard University Press, 1995, 1997)

Vladislav M. Zubok, *A Failed Empire, The Soviet Union In The Cold War From Stalin to Gorbachev,* (Chapel Hill: The University of North Carolina Press, 2007, 2009)